W9-AEO-394

NATURAL LAWN CARE

DOWN-TO-EARTH
NATURAL LAWN CARE

DICK RAYMOND

A Storey Publishing Book

STOREY

Storey Communications, Inc.
Pownal, Vermont 05261

Cover design by Wanda Harper Joyce
Cover art by Carol Jessop
Cover and interior photographs by Paul Boisvert
Photos on pages 78 and 79 (top) courtesy of John Deere & Co.
Photos on pages 130 and 131 courtesy of Gardener's Supply
Line drawings by Alison Kolesar
Drawings on pages 16 and 22 by Elayne Sears; on pages 126 and 128 by Judy Eliason; on page 132 by
Charles Joslin; on pages 138 and 140 by Hyla Scudder; on pages 141 and 142 by Mallory Lake
Text design by Cindy McFarland and Meredith Maker
Production by Meredith Maker

Edited by Dave Schaefer and Ben Watson
Indexed by Nan Badgett, Word•a•bil•i•ty

Copyright © 1993 by Storey Communications, Inc.

*The information in this book is true and complete to the best of our knowledge. All recommendations are made without
guarantee on the part of the author or Storey Communications, Inc. The author and publisher disclaim any liability in
connection with the use of this information. For additional information, please contact Storey Communications, Inc.,
Schoolhouse Road, Pownal, Vermont 05261.*

Printed in the United States by Courier

First Printing, January 1993

Library of Congress Cataloging-in-Publication Data

Raymond, Dick.
    Down-to-Earth natural lawn care / Dick Raymond.
            p.   cm.
    "A Storey Publishing book."
    Includes bibliographical references and index.
    ISBN 0-88266-812-9 (hc) — ISBN 0-88266-810-2 (pbk.)
    1. Lawns.   2. Organic gardening.   I. Title.   II. Title: Natural lawn care.
SB433.R38   1992
635.9'647 — dc20   92-53950
                                                             CIP

CONTENTS

INTRODUCTION
YOUR LAWN
AT WORK FOR YOU

I'VE BEEN WORKING with grasses ever since I can remember. While growing up on a farm, our grass was always considered a crop unto itself. The hay that fed the livestock was and is one of a dairy farmer's essential crops.

Today, on my 55-acre homestead, I have 35 acres of lawn, including a 12-hole golf course I have been building as a research project. Parks and golf courses are places where people tend to spend a lot of time in close contact with the turf grasses. So I've been experimenting with large-scale techniques for reducing overuse of chemicals by blending fertilizers and using alternatives to pesticides and fungicides.

Many people say that watching grass grow is one of the most boring activities known to man. I disagree. Turf grasses are constantly changing and reacting to the conditions around them. Even more important, they work hard by standing still. Most of us don't appreciate what our everyday lawn of turf grass is actually doing. Let's look at some examples.

Lawns Help Keep Us Sneeze-Free

Lawns help people with allergies in two ways. First, where there are no lawns, weeds take over

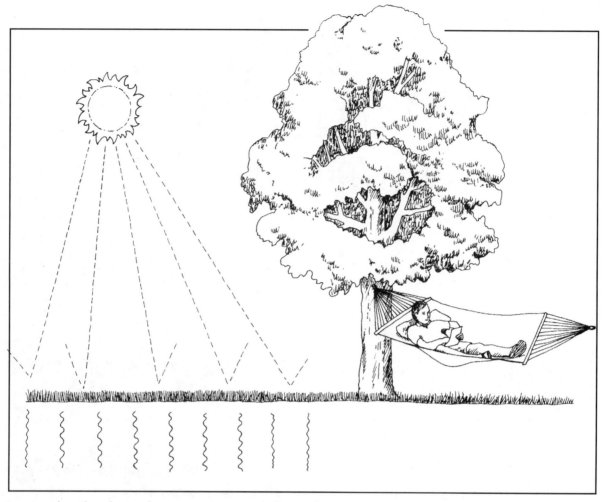

Lawns absorb solar radiation and scatter light, making grassy areas feel cooler and more comfortable on hot, sunny days.

and start their cycle of producing pollen. Lawns will not produce pollen if they are kept mowed. Second, lawns act like sponges to catch and recycle airborne dust, pollen, and spores.

Lawns Are Nature's Air Conditioners

Lawns help us to keep cool in the summer. They absorb solar radiation and convert it to plant growth. On a hot, sunny summer day, try standing with one foot on a sandy beach or asphalt pavement, and the other on a patch of lawn and you'll get the idea. The temperature over a lawn will be from 10 to 14 degrees cooler than over concrete or asphalt. On extremely hot days, it can approach 30 degrees. Research has demonstrated that, on a block with eight average houses, front lawns have the cooling effect of about 70 tons of air conditioning!

While grass absorbs some of the sun's radiation and converts it into growth, it also scatters light and radiation. Glare, reflection, and evaporation are reduced, which, in turn, creates a cooling effect. Lawns and gardens, especially the shady spots, are favorite places to

Whoever said that lawns all have to look the same? On my property, the lawn links trees, buildings, vegetable gardens — even a pond fringed with cattails and wildflowers — into the overall landscape design.

be on hot days. That's when the effort you've put into them really pays you back.

Lawns Help Clean Up Water Supplies

Turf grasses are highly efficient pollution processors. The federal Clean Air Act came about because millions of tons of pollutants are spewed into the air every day from cars, factories, homes, and utilities. As pollutants are brought to earth by rain and snow or simply filter down, they are captured in the grass, dissolved in water and broken down by soil microbes into harmless materials. Chemical fertilizers and pesticides are also broken down in the life cycle of turf grasses. Many golf courses use sewage effluent on turf, which cleans it and keeps it away from other water sources. Perhaps some day we will see plants being used to clean up municipal sewage.

In addition, high acidity in rainwater can be reduced tenfold after being filtered through grasses. Applying ground limestone to turf grasses helps to neutralize these acids, too.

Grasses help to keep water pure in another

way, as well. They reduce runoff. Water that runs across asphalt and concrete picks up all kinds of pollutants and deposits them somewhere else — usually in another body of water. Turf grasses help to capture this polluted water, even on slopes.

Lawns Fight Air Pollution

Plants absorb gasses through their leaves, and a lawn is are made up of millions of individual grass leaves. Grass converts the gasses and releases them as oxygen. They also absorb vehicle emissions such as carbon dioxide, as well as nasty pollutants like sulfur dioxide, ozone, hydrogen fluoride, and peroxyacetyl nitrate. An acre of healthy turf grass is capable of absorbing hundreds of pounds of sulfur dioxide per year. The next time you see those green belts along highways you can think of them as air-filtration factories.

Lawns Add to Your Peace and Quiet

Lawns absorb sound with about the same efficiency as a heavy carpet on a felt pad. Along with other ornamental plants, they reduce undesirable noise levels by 20 to 30 percent. They also encourage the presence of pleasant sounds, like birds.

Lawns Show Off Your Home

If you drive through a brand-new development, it will seem awfully bare, and the houses will all tend to look alike. But if you come back after the lawns and landscapes are established, it's a very different scene. A well-planned landscape will use the lawn to connect various elements. You can use it to distinguish your home from all the others, and in the past few years the number of people involved in landscaping has increased dramatically.

Lawns Are a Good Investment

Studies have shown that many people equate a tidy, thriving lawn with success. Your lawn and landscape are the first things people see when they come and the last things they see when they leave — an important consideration when you are selling a home. Landscaping may be the best investment you can make when it comes to getting a return on your home improvement dollar, sometimes returning between 100 to 200 percent.

Lawns Control Erosion

This might sound insignificant, but many years ago I drove through a city in Canada where smelting operations had destroyed all the vegetation downwind for several miles. There was no carpet of grass to provide all the positive benefits previously discussed, or to prevent erosion. The landscape looked like the surface of the moon. Hillsides had been chewed away by rains, while swampy mud flats developed in low areas, dotted with polluted puddles. I have never forgotten that scene. Wind and water never stop working on bare soil. Grasses, however, hold the soil in place and deep-rooted grasses like alfalfa are sometimes planted to prevent steep banks from eroding away.

One of the lawn's most important functions is as an "outside room" — an area for playing games or entertaining guests. The grass varieties you choose to plant in these areas should be able to handle heavy traffic.

Lawns Are Ideal Places to Play and Entertain

From the backyard cookout to the game of catch, lawns perform an important social function as "outdoor rooms" during those seasons when people prefer to be outside.

Where would sports be without turf grass? Golf, football, tennis, soccer, baseball, and other sports around the world rely on turf grass. We don't do much jousting any more (at least not in my neck of the woods!), but lawns began with games and tournaments and will always be an important part of the world of sports. What does all this mean to us? Love your lawn.

CHAPTER 1

HEALTHY LAWN,
HEALTHY LIFE

I CONSIDER MYSELF LUCKY to have spent most of my life trying out new ways to have better, more bountiful gardens. Those 50 years of gardening experience have convinced me of something I suspected even when I was a youngster on the farm; namely, you have to know the difference between those things that are important and necessary to do and those that don't need to be done at all. I believe a certain kind of laziness makes great sense. Let nature do most of the work.

This book is all about working with nature rather than against it. If you follow these methods, I can promise you'll have a healthy, great-looking lawn with less work, expense, and wear and tear on the environment. If you're doubtful, let me give you a few examples.

❧ Shampoo your lawn with household soap and you can probably forget about common insect and disease problems that require strong chemical cures.

❧ Apply too much nitrogen fertilizer and you will only have to mow your lawn more often. As much as half of the fertilizer isn't even necessary or useful to the grass, but you're still paying for it. Excess nitrogen can also cause thatch, which means you will have to spend time and energy removing it or pay someone else to do it.

❧ One of the least expensive garden supplies — lime — could be more important to your lawn than a bag of the most expensive fertilizer. In this book, I'm going to tell you how to know what your lawn really needs to thrive.

❧ Knowing how and when to mow your lawn can actually eliminate some kinds of weeds over a few seasons, without the need for chemicals.

❧ Planting the right kind of grass in the

If you live in the East or the Pacific Northwest, lime may be the most important substance you can put on your lawn. Lime sweetens acid soils, and only when the soil's pH is balanced in the 6.5 to 7.5 range can grass plants fully "digest" the nutrients in the fertilizer you apply during the year.

right place can make the difference between an easy, successful lawn and one that never looks good.

Lawns and grasses play a big part in people's lives. I think there's nothing better than a beautiful lawn, landscape, and garden around a house. Even in neighborhoods where every house looks pretty much the same, the one with a carefully-thought-out and well-cared-for lawn and landscape will stand out and look special.

A lawn is a place for our children and grandchildren to play. It helps keep our homes cool and quiet. It is an environmental workhorse that filters out a lot of airborne pollu-

tion before it can reach the soil and get into our water supply. And dozens of games (including my favorite one, golf) depend on a turf lawn as a playing field.

People often ask me, "How did we go so far wrong that we've turned our lawns into health hazards?" A more important question is, "How do we get back to making lawns the beautiful and healthy surroundings they should be?"

I would answer that a lawn is something like a forest — a forest of grass with many billion more plants than there are trees in the world. Forests grow, mature, die, and replenish themselves without any help from mankind. Why? Because they are a closed cycle — one that relies on moisture, nutrients in the soil, and the energy of the sun. The trees send down roots, gather up the nutrients, take in energy from the sun and drop leaves or needles that are recycled back into the ground to become nutrients once again. No one provides extra fertilizer or sprays. Diseases are rare and usually attack the weakest of the species as part of the life and death cycle of nature. Even an infestation of gypsy moths rarely destroys a healthy forest.

Just like forest ecosystems, grasses throughout the world can get along perfectly well without us. In fact, the great prairies of this country were much healthier before people came along and interfered with them.

Where we have gone wrong is in thinking we have to get on a monthly schedule of fertilization and pesticide/herbicide application as a preventive measure. It's overkill. Not only do we pour on too many chemicals, but we also make unnecessary work for ourselves and spend too much money in the process. It's the same old story; instead of understanding and working with nature, we try to control it. In the long run, that's a mistake.

However, I don't believe that every chemical is necessarily "wrong" and every so-called natural solution is necessarily "right." I use chemicals sparingly when I have an exceptionally tough problem and I don't feel guilty about it at all. Chemical fertilizers often originate as mineral deposits that are then mined for use. The problem with chemical fertilizers is not where they come from, but how we use them.

We've also been led to believe that all "natural" pest controls are gentle. That's not necessarily the case. The natural pesticide nicotine sulfate, derived from the tobacco plant and sold for years as Black Leaf 40, is 1,300 times more toxic than the chemical malathion. Organic insecticides like rotenone and the pyrethrins have shorter active lives than many chemicals, but are still quite potent and can be toxic to fish. Moderation and good judgment must be exercised when using any chemical — regardless of whether it's synthetic or naturally derived.

I think many American homeowners have been misled about the correct way to care for a lawn. That's understandable. In some parts of the country lawn care is almost a competitive sport, and a weedy, shabby lawn can create a lot of pressure from the neighbors to

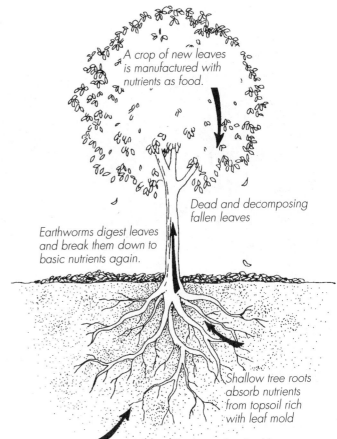

A crop of new leaves is manufactured with nutrients as food.

Dead and decomposing fallen leaves

Earthworms digest leaves and break them down to basic nutrients again.

Shallow tree roots absorb nutrients from topsoil rich with leaf mold

Minerals that are available in subsoil are absorbed by deep tree roots

Just like the trees in a forest, a healthy lawn is a natural ecosystem — a forest of grass. Soil life like earthworms break down a tree's fallen leaves and enrich the soil. In much the same way, grass clippings and other organic matter are broken down by living organisms in a healthy lawn into nutrients that the roots of grass can absorb and feed to the plants.

shape up. All too often the response has been the quick fix — just pour on the miracle chemicals that will make everything all right.

A Little Lawn History

In some ways I think we're lucky to have lawns at all. At one time, they were only for the wealthy who could afford peasants to care for them.

One of the earliest turf sports, lawn bowling, remains popular in Great Britain and other parts of the world.

Early medieval lawns were used for games and tournaments, much as they are today. Specific directions for creating a lawn with sod go back to about 1306, and they aren't much different from the techniques used now, although medieval lawns were only "mowed" twice a year. The cutting of these early lawns was done by men with scythes, and women came along behind to gather up the grass. They were sometimes called "sporting greenplots" and were reserved for the recreation of the privileged classes. Today we have golf courses and athletic fields of all kinds. We have even invented artificial grass on which we play many sports.

One sport that has changed, however, is bowling. We don't have many bowling greens in this country any more, but the original place and name still remain in Ohio and Kentucky. The sport of lawn bowling is still popular in some parts of the world, though, with Southampton, England, claiming to have the oldest green, laid down sometime before 1299.

As time went on, scenic turf walkways were created in England for women and men to take romantic strolls on pleasant afternoons. The tradition continued, and here in rural New England, some folks still snicker when a young couple is teased about being off "grassing."

By the early 1700s, the landscaped garden had become an integral part of every fashionable mansion, and turf mowing became more important. Edges were sheared and lawns were rolled by man or horse power (the horses wore woolen mufflers on their feet to protect the lawn). The meadows were mowed as grazing animals moved back away from the house. By the late 1700s, people were gathering seeds from prime upland meadows and starting lawns with them, although moving turf remained the favorite means of starting a new lawn.

In the early 1800s, as the availability of cheap labor declined, lawns began shrinking in size. Then, in 1830, the lawn mower was invented, and it changed things forever. Suddenly, almost anyone could have a lawn.

I always enjoy the story of how the lawn mower was invented because I have invented machines for lawn and garden use myself. The lawn mower was invented by Thomas Budding, an engineer in the textile trade, where a cylinder of spiraled blades was used to trim the nap of cloth. It must have been an exciting discovery when he saw how the nap of cloth and grass were alike. Before long he had invented the reel lawn mower. Seventy years later, at the beginning of this century, someone fitted a gasoline engine to a lawn mower. Thus came another breakthrough — the rotary mower — which now far outnumbers all other types. And, more recently, the riding mower has become very popular with lawn owners. Finally we have a substitute for the peasants.

The rise of the gasoline engine and the decline of the horse had a major impact on gardening. Horse manure, once the basic horticultural fertilizer, became far less plentiful, and, at the same time, researchers found that plant growth was based on three basic chemicals: nitrogen, phosphorus, and potassium. The use of animal fertilizers gave way to chemical mixtures. The shift took place quickly, beginning in this country in the late 1800s. The first mixed fertilizer was patented in 1849 in Baltimore, Maryland. Rock phosphate deposits were being mined in South Carolina in 1867. Potash deposits were being mined in Carlsbad, New Mexico, in 1931. Nitrates were imported from Chile.

Life changed a lot after the beginning of the twentieth century. The family farm declined and people moved to the cities, but many found they could still grow a lawn. After War War II, however, everyone wanted a house and a yard in the suburbs. Chemical fertilizers gave new lawns fast results, and chemical pesticides worked like a miracle on all those nasty bugs. By the year 2000 pesticide manufacturers are expected to ship 1.3 billion pounds of pesticides worth $19 billion. Some 67 million pounds a year end up on lawns in the United States alone.

As these early engravings show, lawn care is hardly a recent phenomenon. Some equipment, like the roller (top) hasn't changed much over the years. Other labor-saving devices, like these early lawn mowers (center and bottom), have become more efficient and easier to handle.

An Important Number to Know

Keep this number handy for emergencies and to get reliable answers to your pesticide questions.

Call 1-800-858-PEST for answers to your pesticide questions. This is the 24-hour National Pesticide Telecommunications Hotline in service 365 days a year.

The service is sponsored by the Environmental Protection Agency and the Texas Tech University Health Sciences Center School of Medicine.

Hopefully, you won't have to access it under the same circumstances that many people call — on referral from a poison control center because a youngster has swallowed a pesticide.

The hotline has the results of the latest studies from the EPA and other groups and is neither pro or con about pesticides. You can find out how a pesticide works, how long it lasts, what is known about its short- and long-term health risks, its effects and symptoms, and what is likely to be a lethal dose.

During the height of the summer growing season, the hotline gets up to 300 calls a day. If it's busy, the people are likely to answer, "Pesticide information, is this a medical emergency?" and you may be placed on hold so they can take a priority call. They also field most questions on pesticides and pets.

The Chemical-Dependent Lawn

Today, homeowners use between 5.3 and 10.6 pounds of pesticides per acre per year on their lawns, which is many times the amount per acre generally used by farmers. Homeowners are neither licensed nor trained in pesticide application and seem to be victims of the idea that if a little is good, more is better. This has proven to be very faulty — and potentially dangerous — logic. Now, some side effects are cropping up that have given us a scare.

The concern has come about as an increasing number of children, pets, athletes, and gardeners have reported strange symptoms including troubled breathing, loss of weight and appetite, skin irritations and burns, headaches, muscle aches and fever, and swelling. Pesticide and herbicide ingredients are being blamed. However, some experts deny these claims altogether, while others hold that these people are just very sensitive to chemicals. No one is really sure. As a result of all the publicity, though, more and more people are asking themselves, "Why take the chance?"

The point I'd like to make is this: relying on chemicals to have a great-looking lawn isn't necessary. In fact, it's downright silly. You can use less, work less, spend less, and stay healthy while still maintaining a terrific lawn.

Today we have the Environmental Protection Agency to oversee the use of toxic chemicals. However, the fact is there are chemicals currently on the market that have been approved, but not tested, by the EPA. The testing program of active ingredients in pesticides continues, but it is not expected to be completed until 1997 at the earliest.

The effects of some chemicals take time to be recognized. Also, some pesticides move up through the food chain — from bug to bird, for example — and pose a serious threat to wildlife.

Ironically, we import large quantities of vegetables into the United States from other nations, where pesticides like DDT — long banned in this country — continue to be used. In addition to the health questions that have been raised, there is also evidence that long-term use of pesticides may be creating so-called "superbugs." These superbugs develop immunities to typical pesticide applications and require larger and larger doses to kill them.

Facts About Fertilizers

Pesticides, herbicides, and fungicides are often grouped together with chemical fertilizers, but there are important differences. In my opinion, the primary negative factor about chemical fertilizers is that, ironically, they can be too effective.

Plants absorb fertilizer gradually. Unfortunately, up to half the amount of a typical chemical fertilizer is wasted because it leaches through the soil or runs off before the plants can absorb its nutrients. Also, fertilizers can create a secondary problem when they run off into waterways and stimulate the growth

Taking a core sample of your lawn can indicate its general state of health. Plants should have deep root systems like the core second from left, so the grass can reach deep down for water and nutrients. Too much fibrous material above the soil, as in the core on the right, means that thatch may be starving your grass and inviting disease and insect damage.

The soil is the best place to start when you want to improve the looks of your lawn. Determining what kind of soil structure you have — clay, sand, or loam — and getting the soil tested will tell you a lot about what steps you'll need to take in future.

of undesirable water plants. This is more of a problem with agricultural plants, but you should bear it in mind if you live near a lake, river, or pond. Research published by the Minnesota Extension Service reports that lawn pesticide leaching (passing through the soil) and runoff have the potential to harm water supplies, even though lawns are generally successful at filtering chemicals and pollen.

Finally, the use of strong chemical fertilizers can produce the opposite results of those we want for our lawns. They can encourage thatch, lower resistance to pests, and encourage superficial foliage growth at the expense of deep, healthy root growth that will resist drought. An example is nitrogen, which is an important fertilizer for grass, as it is for all leafy plants. Too much nitrogen, however, encourages the formation of thatch. Thatch is a layer of plant matter above the soil that prevents water and fertilizer from reaching plant roots. It can also mean you have to mow your lawn more often. Don't make more work for yourself! (See Chapter 5 on fertilization, and the section on thatch in Chapter 7, page 95.)

Lessons from nature are the basis for the chapters to follow. Following nature's example will help you build a strong, healthy lawn that will survive tough times. I'm convinced that it's easy to get back on the right track. We can begin by understanding a little about how nature works, and then try to work along with it. That's what the rest of this book is all about.

Human nature being what it is, I would guess that you'll turn first to the seasonal guide to lawn maintenance to see what you should be doing this month. That's okay, as long as you don't skip over the chapter on soil. Just as you can't erect a solid building on a shaky foundation, so, too, all successful lawns and gardens must start with healthy, living soil. When I called this book "down-to-earth," I wasn't kidding.

Timing is everything. Every farmer can tell you that in this part of the country you plant in the spring and harvest in the fall. Stated that simply, you might believe that's all there is to farming. The reality is that there's a right time to plant, a right time to mow, a right time to fertilize, and a right time to leave well enough alone and go fishing or play golf. So don't forget to check the maintenance calendar.

Lawn insects and diseases seem like a mystery to many people, but chances are most lawns will have just one or two problems — not everything in the book. The secret is knowing what you're up against so you don't blast everything in sight (or out of sight). The same is true of weeds. Some definitions of weeds are a matter of taste. Lighten up a little.

Throughout this book you'll find a lot of my favorite tips and tricks about starting new lawns and caring for existing ones. And you can bet they'll be the most labor-saving approaches I've found.

Choosing the right seeds for a new lawn will save you a lot of work. If you have an existing lawn, you can overseed it with another variety without tearing it up and starting over. In the South, overseeding lets you have a green lawn during the winter when the lawn would usually turn brown. That's a trick that's used at southern golf courses to keep them green all year long. (See the chapters on seed varieties, the maintenance calendar, and the section on overseeding.)

I hope you enjoy this book and the basic philosophy behind it: Use less, work less, spend less, take it easy on the environment, but still have great results!

CHAPTER 2

GIVE YOUR LAWN
A PHYSICAL

I BELIEVE THERE ARE two kinds of lawn owners in the world. One kind doesn't want to spend time fooling with the lawn, isn't particularly interested in how lawns or other living things "work," and is happy to pay someone else to keep it green — no questions asked. The other kind of lawn owner, however, is more environmentally curious and aware. This kind of person actually enjoys working on lawns and gardens and views his or her property as a strand in the web of life. The processes of life and growth are fascinating to such a person. What's more, I'll bet you are one of these people, or you wouldn't be reading this book right now. So allow me to share my number one secret of gardening success with you.

If 50 years of gardening experience have taught me one thing, it is this: take care of the soil and nearly everything else will be all right. The soil is the foundation of life itself and from it springs all living things. When I began to research organic lawn care on my homemade golf course, I knew the same thing was true. You eventually will succeed if you think of the soil first.

The soil and dirt are two very different things. Dirt is what you find under your bed when you don't clean often enough. But soil is alive — a busy factory that produces much of what plants need to survive. If your lawn is a beautiful, lush, green carpet you can be sure that healthy soil helped to get it off to a good start. On the other hand, if problems are showing up on the surface, you can probably trace them back to what is happening down in the soil out of sight.

The lawn is typically the last item on the list when a new house is being built. The building debris is bulldozed in around the foundation, and a few truckloads of topsoil are hauled in to cover up the hard soil that has been pulled out of the cellar excavation. A few pounds of bargain grass seed are scattered around, cov-

RELATIVE SIZE OF SOIL GRAINS

LIGHT SOILS	HEAVY SOILS	
MEDIUM SAND	VERY FINE SAND	FINE SILT
FINE SAND	COARSE SILT	CLAY

ered with straw, and that's the lawn.

After a few years, though, the problems start to appear. It's at this point that many people are tempted to apply the latest chemical miracle. However, that's not the best solution. And, all too often, we only compound the problem by catching all the grass clippings in a bag and then setting them out on the curb to fill up our landfills. Nowadays, most landfills will not even accept yard wastes or, if they do, they make you pay a penalty. Clippings should be left on the lawn to build soil right where they were cut. I'll also tell you how to compost these wastes in Chapter 7.

Here are some factors that will shape the success of your lawn and garden: depth, fertility, texture, and structure.

Depth

The best soils will be several feet deep. Sometimes you won't know the situation of your own soil without digging a hole two or three feet deep. When you do, some of the problems you might find are:

❧ Ledge, with just a few inches of soil on top of it. If you look around a property built on ledge you will usually see rocky outcroppings sticking up from the surface, and there's a good chance that any building will have its foundation sitting on top of the ledge, not built into it. A friend of mine who has ledge on his property told me that he once put a running hose down and noticed it formed a small hole, but no puddle. Upon digging deeper, he saw that the water was running into a crack in the buried ledge and then away to who knows where.

❧ Hardpan. This is a hard layer of soil a few inches thick just a foot or two under the ground. It causes drainage problems. Sometimes you can break it up with a pick or crowbar, but you might have to install a drainage system.

❧ A buried boulder, left behind by the glaciers and covered over. It can cause a mystery dry spot if it is just below the surface.

❧ Clay. Some clays are like concrete when they dry out but still support grasses on the top four to eight inches of topsoil.

Fertility

The fertility of your lawn depends upon the chemistry of your soil, including the nutrients found there and the degree to which the soil is acid, alkaline, or nearly neutral.

Texture

You can learn a lot about the texture of your soil from the squeeze test and the jar test described on page 21. Texture is determined by the relative amounts of sand, silt, and clay particles in your soil. (See drawing on page 16.)

Structure

The air space between the soil particles determines whether the soil will drain properly and be able to retain moisture and nutrients.

How to Look at Your Lawn

I keep notes on my lawn and garden. I turn these notes into a plan and then turn that plan into a monthly calendar of times when gardening tasks should be done. For example, every New Year's Day I go down in the basement and find the geraniums I pulled out and stored in brown paper bags. Then I trim them back and repot them, because they will start greening up in January, right inside the paper bag. It's a little look ahead toward spring at the coldest time of the year.

I'd like to take you on a little tour of my lawn, because it will help you to look at your own lawn, make a plan, and then act on it.

The first thing to remember is that your lawn should be what you and your family want it to be, not necessarily the manicured carpet you see in advertisements. No lawn should be too perfect for kids to play on, and it certainly shouldn't be so full of chemicals that you wonder if it's safe for them to play on.

I look at my lawn as if it were divided into two different kinds of zones. One zone is related to how we use the lawn, and the other involves the natural features that will influence how the grass grows. These natural features include sun, shade, wet, dry, soil types, steep banks, etc.

Here are some of the use zones at my home:

❦ Cook-out and entertaining area near the house. Here we need grass that will stand up to occasional hard use. This area is mostly sunny and nearly flat.

❦ Working lawns around the vegetable gardens. These are the lanes to and from the gardens, and they get a lot of traffic from power equipment and carts, hoses being dragged over them, etc. They need a durable grass. This area has full sunshine and is flat.

❦ Approach to the house. The view coming in the driveway is the setting for our home. This is our front yard and we want it to be attractive. This area gets full sunshine and is gently rolling.

❦ Exposed hilltops. They get full sun and are the first places to dry out. The soil in these areas needs extra organic matter to retain moisture.

❦ Hillsides in full sun. I want to encourage solid root growth here to hold the soil. If I'm not careful, I can scalp the lawn while mowing the contours.

🌸 Shady areas on the north side of buildings and hillsides and areas in and around the trees. These areas need a grass that will tolerate shade — some more than others, depending upon their exposure.

🌸 Steep, wooded bank. This is an area for a ground cover other than grass. The largest one on my property is covered with daylilies.

🌸 Golf greens. These are the only areas of bent grass on the property.

🌸 Fairways in the flood plain. This is a moist, low-lying area and can be hit by diseases. It is mostly sunny.

🌸 Fairways on high ground. These are flat and sunny, and they have a lot of white clover in the mix.

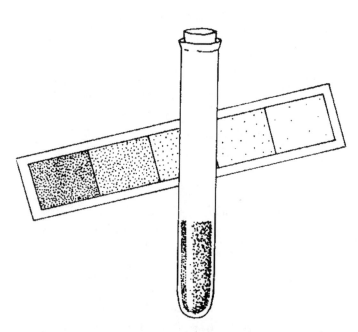

A home test kit is a simple and inexpensive way to test the pH of your soil.

🌸 Evergreen plantings. Although there are other houses nearby, none of them can be seen from our house. These plantings and selective tree removal are the reason. A shady grass mix is best under trees.

🌸 Ponds. Marsh plants, like cattails, help to keep the water pure. Because we live in the country, we like to have a pond near the house for reasons of fire protection. Since our living room, dining room, and deck overlook the pond, I sometimes surround it with a ground cover of annual wildflowers.

Even though you probably don't have this many zones, most homes, even on small city lots, have some or most of the following types of zones:

1. A front lawn facing the street that frames the house and that should look rich, healthy, and well-kept.

2. A few shady areas on the north side of the house and garage, or under trees.

3. A problem area where the lawn is thin or weedy — probably both.

4. An area used for play, entertaining, or both, that needs extra durability.

You might find it helpful, at this point, to get a sheet of graph paper and make a little map of your property and its zones. Using Chapter 9 on year-round maintenance, you can find out the best times to fertilize, overseed, repair, and make other improvements. Using Chapter 4, you can choose the best grass for the job, and Chapter 7 will tell you how to do it. If you have problems with weeds, insects, or a lawn disease, chapters 6, 10, and 11 will help you to find a solution.

And remember, the path to a healthy, beautiful lawn can be as simple as doing the right thing at the right time. That does not always mean reaching for a box or bag of chemicals.

Get Outside, Take a Look

Let's begin by giving the soil in your lawn a physical. Don't flip to another chapter. This is the most important step and, once you un-derstand it, you'll have the key to creating a great lawn and a great garden, too.

I recommend doing two tests. One shows the makeup of the soil and the other indicates what nutrients the soil has and what it lacks.

Here's what you'll need:

☙ a trowel or spade

☙ a non-metallic bucket

☙ a glass jar and lid

☙ a soil-test kit

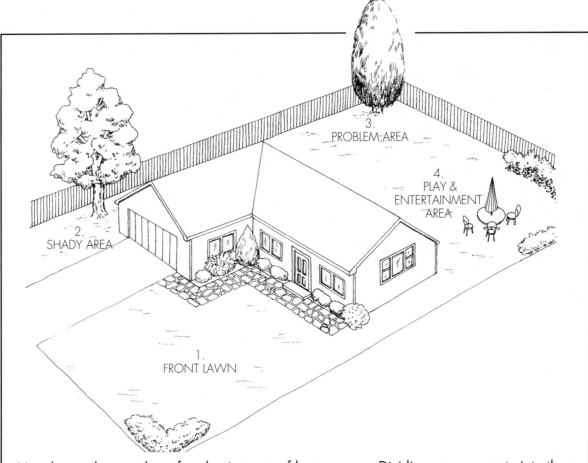

3.
PROBLEM AREA

4.
PLAY &
ENTERTAINMENT
AREA

2.
SHADY AREA

1.
FRONT LAWN

Most homes have at least four basic types of lawn zones. Dividing your property into these different activity and growing areas can help you in selecting the right grass or ground cover for each location.

Before you can improve your soil, you'll first need to have a soil test done. Take several samples from each of the different areas of your lawn, using a sharp spade (left). While you're at it, take a close look at the grass itself (right); if you notice more than a half inch of fibrous material lying on top of the soil, you may need to dethatch and aerate your lawn.

If you have a large property or one that has very different types of areas within it, you should treat each area separately. For example, the highest part of the property may have different soil from the lowest.

Next, check at your local garden center for a soil-test kit. In most states, the Cooperative Extension Service at the state university offers a soil-testing service. Among the 25 northern states, only one state university (Illinois) does not do soil tests. If the service is not available through the university, you may have to look for an independent soil-testing laboratory. Your garden center should know how to locate the laboratory in your area.

Some test kits sold over the counter simply tell you, through a color test, the relative acidity or alkalinity (pH) of your soil. This is important information for improving lawn and garden soil, but it does not give a complete picture of your soil's nutrient content. This simple litmus test will tell you if you need to add lime, which is usually the case east of the Mississippi, or sulphur, which is the case in much of the West.

A complete soil test will not only tell you about alkalinity, but will also cover phosphorus, potassium, and soil texture. It may even get into other nutrients, like nitrogen. (See Chapter 5 on fertilization for instructions about how to use the tests.)

To take the tests, dig a hole six to seven inches deep, cutting out the sod carefully so it can be replaced later. With a spade or trowel, take a half-inch slice of soil from the edge of the hole, top to bottom. Then take a half-inch cross section — top to bottom — of the slice. Put this sample into a bucket. Repeat this process in a dozen or more places, up to 20, until you have samples from all parts of your property. If you have an area that is obviously different from the others, treat it as a separate zone and take enough samples from the area to provide a broad range. Mix up the soil from similar areas in the bucket. Keep a written record of which samples came from which different areas. You will need about a pint of soil for each soil test, so make sure you take enough samples.

Different types of soil have different structures. Take a handful of soil from the hole. If it is clay, you can squeeze it in your hand and

form a ball that will hold its shape (after all, clay is used to make pottery). A ball of sandy soil will crumble and not hold its shape. Loam will form a ball but crumble easily with a little pressure from your thumb.

Next, put about three inches of soil in a glass jar (or jars if you are testing different areas), and cover it with two inches of water. Cover the jar tightly. Then shake it up and let it stand overnight. This is a simple test that will show you something about the make-up of your soil.

In the morning, take a look. Sticks and dry grass will be floating on the surface, but the layers you see at the bottom will tell you a lot about the soil. At the top will be decomposed organic matter, then clay, then silt, then sand and finally gravel. You may not have every layer. What does this tell you?

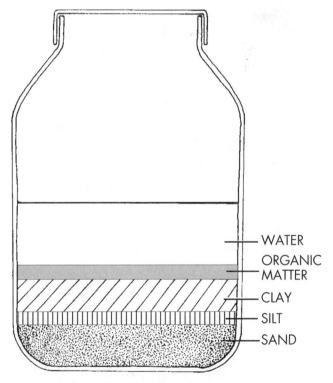

WATER
ORGANIC MATTER
CLAY
SILT
SAND

A simple home jar test can tell you a lot about the structure of your soil.

Look at the layer below the organic matter:

- If it is 35 to 50 percent clay, you have heavy clay soil.

- If it is 25 to 30 percent clay, you have clay soil.

- If it is 10 to 20 percent clay, you have a medium loam.

- If it is 5 to 10 percent clay, you have a sandy loam.

- If it is less than 5 percent clay, your soil is sandy.

Soils have both texture and structure based on the sizes of the particles of which they are made.

Press some soil together in the palm of your hand. On sandy or poor soils the particles won't adhere at all. Soil with a high clay content will form a compact ball. But loamy, rich soil with plenty of organic matter (the kind all of us would like to have) will form a loose ball that will break with a touch of your finger.

Clay. Sometimes called "heavy" soil, clay is made up of the smallest of particles — too small for the eye to see. It is difficult to work with because, when moist, the tiny particles bind together to form great clumps. It is slow to warm up in the spring and delays garden planting. There is little air in clay. When it dries, the surface of the soil will crack and water will run off, rather than in. In the Southwest, gardeners deal with a white clay called *caliche* that is so tough they sometimes treat it like an in-ground flowerpot. They excavate a hole, fill it with peat moss and other organic matter, and plant. For all its disadvantages, clay does do a good job of storing nutrients and can be quite productive.

Silt. Particles are larger than clay but smaller than sand.

Sand. These particles are visible and can vary widely in size. Sandy soils are easy to work, but the larger the particles, the faster water and nutrients run right through the grains. Also, they will dry out quickly.

Loam. Every gardener wants, but few have, loamy soil. Loam contains a combination of clay, silt, and sand. It allows air to penetrate, but still holds water and nutrients.

A soil with good structure allows air, moisture, and nutrients to work together in balance to promote healthy plant growth and healthy growth of the living soil.

All soils can be improved by adding a lot of organic matter to them in the form of manure, peat moss, compost, or green manures (crops grown just to be turned under). In clay, organic matter breaks up the clumps and allows air to penetrate. In sandy soils, it holds in moisture and binds the soil together. In all soils, it feeds the microscopic plant life.

The easiest way to add organic matter to a lawn is to allow grass clippings to decompose right on the surface every time you mow. This will not cause thatch in healthy soil. Most thatch is caused by using too much nitrogen fertilizer and cutting the lawn too short.

I add organic matter whenever I renovate or repair a lawn. Various types of organic matter are available around the country, ranging from composted leaves to buckwheat and peanut hulls to seaweed. Your garden center can help, but you also might be able to find something at little or no cost that is a by-product of a winery, an apple cider mill, or a husking operation. Be careful about using barnyard manures. Proper composting will create heat and kill weed seeds. But taken straight from the barnyard, manure can bring in unwanted weed seeds that will plague you for years to come.

To improve clay and sand, I work in enough organic matter to visibly change the structure of the top six to eight inches of soil. An ideal mix would be peat moss and compost. Peat moss absorbs up to 20 times its weight in moisture when worked into the soil and breaks down very slowly. Compost provides nutrients and decomposes fairly quickly. One technique is to spread two to three inches of throughly moistened peat moss and compost on the soil and then mix it in. On the negative side, peat moss is expensive and adequate supplies of compost are hard to find. One way to solve the supply problem is to set up your own fertilizer factory and get into backyard composting. (See Chapter 7, page 66.)

The Secret Life of Soil

Each pound of soil is alive with up to 930 billion microorganisms, plus insects and earthworms. Microorganisms are too small to see, but we can all see the earthworms and insects. In healthy soil, they are all hard at work breaking down whatever organic matter is available and converting it to a form that can feed plants. One of the simplest forms of composting is to bury the vegetable wastes from the kitchen in the vegetable garden. In healthy soil, worms and other forms of soil life are so active that all but the toughest materials will disappear in only a few days. And the more organic matter that is fed to the soil, the more active that soil becomes. Organic material like grass clippings will be consumed faster and faster as time goes by, and plants growing on these areas will thrive.

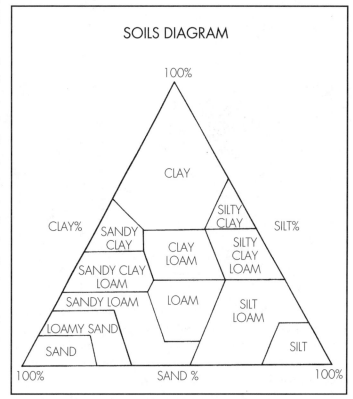

You can see this process for yourself by taking a walk in the woods during the summer. In autumn you were shuffling through fallen leaves several inches thick. By midsummer they were just about all gone. Did someone rake the forests? Yes — essentially, earthworms rake the forest. If you look closely at the ground you can see what has happened. You will find little piles of twigs — the skeletons of the autumn leaves — piled up around tiny, crumbly piles of soil. The earthworms gathered these leaves together around a soil nest in which they laid their eggs. This provided the young earthworms with a meal all ready and waiting for them when they came into the world.

Earthworms are a lawn and garden's best friend. Earthworm manure, called *casts*, is several hundred times richer than the surrounding soil in the basic soil nutrients of nitrogen, phosporus, and potassium. Earthworms digest organic residues, and their tunneling aerates the soil and thus introduces nitrogen. The tunnels go very deep into the soil, especially during dry periods, and help air and water get down below the surface. This, in turn, helps break up heavy soils like clay.

There are a variety of insects active in the soil and, while many are beneficial, some are not. The Japanese beetle, for example, likes well-kept lawns in which to lay its eggs. Those same eggs hatch and become grubs in the soil before emerging as beetles.

Most soil life — fungi, bacteria, algae — is invisible to the naked eye. It's possible to find many types of fungi, all of them competing for food and some feeding on each other. Some of these fungi are responsible for plant diseases. Their purpose is to feed on organic matter and help release nutrients like carbon and nitrogen so that other organisms can use them. In your lawn, grass clippings are broken down and become a major source of nitrogen.

Bacteria break down plant parts into simple components and return them to the soil in a form that plants need for cell synthesis. Algae and nematodes are also part of the invisible zoo in your soil.

All this activity going on in a living soil makes three very important contributions to the health of lawns and gardens:

Did you ever wonder how autumn leaves can disappear so fast? Efficient earthworms are the answer — they pile leaves around their nests and digest the leaves — leaving behind a rich manure called worm castings. No wonder they're such an important part of the soil life in a healthy lawn.

1. Some forms of soil life actually absorb nutrients themselves and pass them along to plants;

2. Some soil life breaks down organic materials into forms the plants can use directly; and,

3. Some organisms transform nitrogen from the air into forms a plant can use. Peas, beans, and clover all form nitrogen nodules among their roots through this *nitrogen-fixing* process.

Most soil life slows down or stops in cold weather. It is most active in its work when the soil temperature is above 70°F (21°C).

What it boils down to is this: organic matter feeds soil life, which in turn feeds plant life. By organic matter I mean material that was once a plant, although many organic fertilizers also contain animal by-products and chemicals found in nature. Perhaps a more technically correct definition of the term *organic* would include all materials based on a carbon structure. Chemicals, particularly when misused, can destroy this vital soil life. And, because chemicals are salts, when overused they can draw moisture out of the plant and cause fertilizer burn. Chemicals work by feeding the plant, not the soil. Think of it this way: you could probably survive for a long time on a diet of vitamin capsules and water. But the most healthy, most vigorous people enjoy a varied and balanced diet and need no vitamins at all. You can feed your soil a similarly balanced diet.

My turf research has had one particular goal in mind: to find an organic fertilizer that would feed the soil and encourage a healthy lawn able to withstand pests, disease, and drought. The fact is just mowing the lawn properly should provide at least half of the fertilizer you need.

CHAPTER 3
WATCHING
YOUR GRASS GROW

WHO SAYS WATCHING GRASS grow is dull? For anyone who has a lawn, knowing how grass grows—and just what kind of grass is growing—can save a lot of time, effort, and money.

This can be achieved by understanding the watering, fertilizing, and mowing needs of various grasses (as well as the diseases that plague them). Then it will be easy for you to have a beautiful and healthy lawn that will grow well with a minimum amount of work, while also being of benefit to the environment. Understanding how grass grows can change your entire outlook on fertilization and help you work with nature and not against it.

Today, the most common grazing animal in populated and suburban America is the lawn mower. It wasn't always that way, of course. Most of our turf grasses trace their origins to the prairie, where they were a food source for grazing animals. Grasses survive to this day because they are different from many other plants. If other plants are mowed or grazed off

almost to the ground, they die, as anyone who has had a woodchuck in the garden knows all too well. But grasses do not grow from their top ends, as most plants do. And that makes all the difference.

The Power of the Crown

Grass grows from a crown that is just above ground level, but low enough to escape the mowers and grazers. Growing right up from the center of the crown is the leaf sheath, which is wrapped around the stem. As the stem grows, the leaf blades unwrap and grow away from the leaf sheath, forming the foliage that most of us think of as "grass."

Since the growth springs from the crown and not the tip, we can cut grass without killing it, as long as we don't cut it too short. Cutting grass too short can damage its ability to provide food for itself. The fertilizer we buy and spread on the lawn does not feed the grass. It simply helps the grass convert moisture and

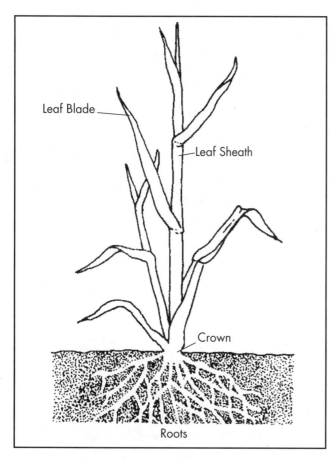

Grasses grow from a crown located just above the surface of the soil. The green leaf blades that we usually think of as "grass" emerge from a leaf sheath that grows up from the center of the crown.

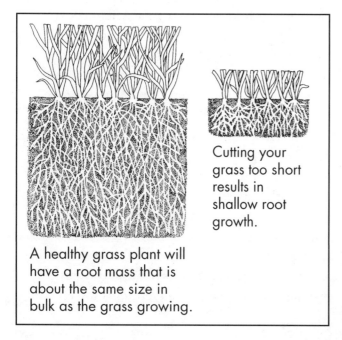

Cutting your grass too short results in shallow root growth.

A healthy grass plant will have a root mass that is about the same size in bulk as the grass growing.

raw materials into food it can use. The leaves of grass create plant food as they use sunlight to convert carbon dioxide from the air into sugars. As these sugars are further converted into protein, fats, and other substances, oxygen is released into the air. This is the process known as *photosynthesis*, which is common to all green plants. It's the very same thing that makes the rain forests so important to the planet as a source of oxygen — yet another way in which your lawn is like a forest. I believe that turf lawns may be even more efficient than forests because they are nearly all foliage. Every 1,000 square feet of lawn (an area just 25 by 40 feet) contains up to a million individual grass plants.

Cutting the lawn too short causes one more thing you don't want to have happen. It can make your lawn shallow-rooted and subject to drought. This is because the more grass that is allowed to grow above the ground, the larger the root mass that will develop underground. Tall grass will produce big healthy root systems, while short grass will produce small, shallow root systems.

Tiny root hairs are constantly probing the soil in search of the moisture and nutrients that support photosynthesis. If these root hairs dry out, your lawn can be seriously damaged. Naturally, a shallow-rooted lawn is more vulnerable to damage and dry conditions than a deep-rooted lawn.

The Root Zone

The top six inches of soil below the crown is called the root zone. This is where the important business of nourishing the plant takes place. Like a busy factory, the soil life is at work producing the nourishment that allows the greenery above to convert sunlight into growth. Grass, as a perennial, builds up organic matter in the soil. Its own clippings, rich in nitrogen, are broken down in this composting/fertilizing/humus-producing factory. The soil is enriched and kept loose. Like the forests, it can operate on its own as a closed system. The decomposing grass and dead grass root material provide food for soil organisms. The organisms in turn convert this material into forms the plant can use as it converts sunlight into growth.

Even if we dig up a section of the root zone we can't see this activity. Some of the soil life exists for just 15 minutes. We can see the results only in a healthy lawn. If we disrupt this process by using chemicals that destroy soil life, the short-term benefits of a lush lawn can result in long-term problems. For example, a heavy dose of high-nitrogen fertilizer will temporarily provide a green lawn at the expense of using up the energy capacity of the root system. A period of dry weather can then stress the grass' growing system, making it weaker and more vulnerable to drought and disease.

By now, vegetable gardeners may think this all sounds a little familiar. Like grass, asparagus also grows from a crown (although it is several inches underground) and it must be allowed to develop a full growth of its fernlike foliage to provide nutrients to the crown and roots for future growth.

Lawns Expand

Watching your grass grow will (if you are patient enough) show you that your lawn wants to spread. It can do this in more than one way, depending upon the type of grass you have.

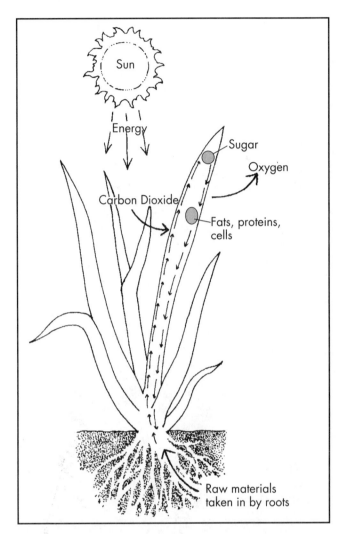

In the process called photosynthesis, the grass plant uses energy from the sun, carbon dioxide from the air, and water and nutrients drawn up from the soil — converting them into simple sugars that the plant needs to grow and releasing oxygen into the air.

Of course, if grass is allowed to go to seed, it will spread seeds that will become new plants if conditions are favorable. Many of our turf grasses come from outstanding examples of wild grass that were collected and allowed to go to seed. In recent years, these varieties have been improved by seedsmen through hybridization.

Individual grass plants expand from the crown by sending out a second shoot, called a

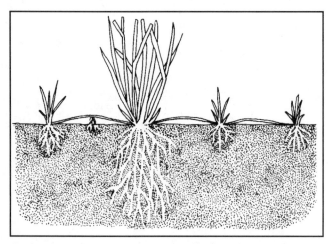

Some grasses propagate themselves by sending out above-ground shoots called stolons, spreading out and establishing new plants as they go. Other types of grasses will self-seed if left uncut.

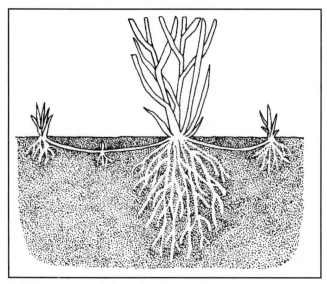

Other spreading grasses expand by means of underground runners, which are called rhizomes.

tiller. This causes the original crown to thicken and spread out. Some grasses use this as the primary means of expansion and are called *bunch grasses* or *clump grasses.* As a vegetable gardener, I'm reminded of the suckers on tomatoes, or the way that broccoli sends out additional shoots after the main stem has been harvested.

Many grasses, including the popular Kentucky bluegrass of the North and the Bermuda grass and Bahia grass of the South, spread by sending out runners that take root and produce a new plant or a series of plants along the runner.

If the runners are underground, they are called *rhizomes,* and if above ground, they are called *stolons.* Some, like Kentucky bluegrass and red fescue, spread by means of underground rhizomes. St. Augustine grass and centipede grass spread by sending out stolons. Others, like Bermuda grass and zoysia grass, send out both rhizomes and stolons.

I take advantage of how grass grows in many ways. Mowing is one, but timing is another. Northern grasses go into their growth spurts in spring and fall, so the time to add lime and fertilizer is spring and fall, with fall being the most important. Lime and organic fertilizers take a while to break down in the soil, so the fall fertilization will really boost spring growth and spring fertilization will boost fall growth. Southern grasses, on the other hand, grow in one peak season when the hot days of summer arrive, so they need frequent summer fertilizations rather than seasonal ones. I also plan to have new lawns in place in time to take advantage of seasonal growth spurts, especially lawns that are planted from sprigs or plugs rather than seeds. Timing will let you take advantage of their natural urge to spread by sending out runners.

Most important, of course, is what happens in the root zone. This is the engine that produces the horsepower that is fired up by the sun and rain that ultimately make plants grow. The more organic matter the root zone has, the better the plants will perform.

CHAPTER 4

IT'S IN THE MIX:

GETTING THE SEEDS YOU NEED

DON'T WAIT until you're all set to plant or repair your lawn before thinking about grass seed. Having a beautiful lawn requires a little more than just throwing some seed on the ground, and seed choices are very important decisions.

Vegetable gardeners get seed catalogs in the mail every year offering a huge selection of varieties for every kind of vegetable. The country is even mapped and divided into climate zones to make it easier to choose the right variety for any climate. But when you go to put in a lawn, you are on your own and can only hope for a knowledgeable staff at the garden center. You may find mixtures marked for sun and others marked for shade. In the fine print you will find a list of the contents, much like the ingredients in the processed food you buy.

Whether you're going to plant a new lawn, renovate an old lawn, or just touch up some bare spots, you really do need to know which grass seed is best for your particular situation. There are many different situations, but we should not make seed selection any more complicated than necessary.

The North

Cool-climate grasses grow well in areas that are covered with snow for at least part of the year. As every northerner with a yard knows, there are growth periods in the cooler weeks of spring and fall. Here you will find Kentucky bluegrass, fine fescue, and bent grass, although you may see a few zoysia grass lawns along more southern coastal areas. With adequate water, the northern grasses will stay green all summer long. Without water, they may appear to be dying, but will snap back with the cool early autumn rains. However, prolonged dry spells can kill them.

The South

The grass varieties found here grow during the hot summer months and become dormant and brown in cooler weather. These lawns look coarse compared to those in the North because they are made up of the wide-bladed grasses like Bahia grass, Bermuda grass, zoysia grass, St. Augustine grass, and centipede grass.

In Between

Where North meets South you may find a mixture of northern and southern grasses depending upon local factors like rainfall, elevation, and exposure to sun and shade. Tall fescues and zoysia grass are the best choices in many areas of this zone, which runs in a band across the country from southern California, east through Oklahoma and Kansas, to the eastern seaboard states of Virginia, the Carolinas, and Georgia. North and west, in the Great Plains, native grasses like buffalo grass and wheatgrass are often used because of their resistance to drought.

Climate is not the only factor to consider. Grass varieties are constantly being improved to bring out their beneficial characteristics. Now you can choose grasses because of their ability to:

❦ tolerate high temperatures

❦ tolerate cold

❦ grow in shady areas

❦ minimize fertilizer use

❦ tolerate drought

❦ tolerate hard use (play areas, sports)

❦ stabilize steep areas

❦ establish a lawn quickly

❦ resist disease and insect infestation

Grasses from around the world can vary widely in their size, shape, and color when allowed to grow completely. As a result, landscapers are using grasses that are allowed to grow to their full height as interesting features in their landscape designs. Some species can tower well over six feet high and set seed plumes. Several of these ornamental grasses are described in Chapter 12.

People who live in areas that have been plagued by long periods of drought may find local grasses that have the ability to survive and can then be incorporated into the home landscape. Droughts in the West and South have created an interest in xeriscaping, which entails building home landscapes with local plants that have stood the test of time and avoiding exotic plants that do well only under ideal circumstances. Local grasses can play a crucial role in this approach, even as ordinary turf lawns fall victim to prolonged droughts and water restrictions.

When I set out to buy grass seed, here are a few things I keep in mind:

1. Not all grasses are perennial (come back year after year). A few are annual and will go through only one growth cycle and then die. A common one is annual rye, which I use in my vegetable garden to follow the last crop of the year. In vegetable gardening it is used as a cover crop and tilled under to help replenish the soil. Annual rye is sown, too, on gardens that will not be in use for a season, to protect them from sprouting a crop of weeds. For lawns, annual rye is often used in a seed mixture because it germinates and grows quickly, providing shade and stabilizing the soil while the slower-germinating bluegrasses get established. Annuals used this way are sometimes called *nurse grasses*. Improved annual ryegrasses also are being used more and more as nurse grasses. I try to find a blend with 5 to 10 percent annual rye, but stay away if the blend includes over 15 or 20 percent. If a blend seems to meet my needs but has no annual rye as a nurse grass, I buy the ryegrass separately and add it. Once you get comfortable with the types of grass that are best suited for various

Find Your Growing Zone

Zone 1: Kentucky bluegrass, bent grass, fescues, and improved ryegrasses. Some zoysia grass in extreme southern and coastal areas.

Zone 2: Bermuda grass, zoysia grass, Bahia grass, St. Augustine grass, and centipede grass. In the most southerly, wet and tropical areas, carpetgrass.

Zone 3: Great Plains native grasses such as buffalo grass, blue grama grass, wheatgrass, and, in some intermountain areas, fine fescues.

Zone 4: Bermuda grass and zoysia grass. In high altitudes, bluegrass and fescues.

Zone 5: Like Zone 1, Kentucky bluegrass, bent grass, fescues, and ryegrass.

purposes, you can make up your own grass-mix recipes.

I always use a mixture of seeds, not just one type. The type of grass best suited for the growing conditions will do well and fill in for the grasses that aren't as well suited. A mixture also helps prevent a disease or insect infestation from sweeping through the lawn, fueled by the weakness of one variety.

2. In the North, a seed mixture may contain bluegrass, annual rye, and fescues. Bluegrass needs nearly full sunshine, but fescues can tolerate partial shade. Nearly every property has a mixture of sun and shade, so these blends take advantage of the fact that different types of grass will "take over," depending upon the conditions in which they are sown.

3. In the South, lawns usually are made up of just one kind of grass. The wide-bladed southern grasses simply crowd out any competitors.

4. There is a trend in grass seeds toward low-maintenance varieties. Thirty years ago there was very little choice: bluegrass in the North, Bermuda grass in the South. The varieties available to homeowners were normally the ones bred for golf courses. As a result, they required the same program of close and frequent mowing, fertilization, and almost constant management. New varieties, however, may grow lower, more slowly, and require less fertilization.

All grass seeds are not created equal — each variety grows best in different regions of the country or under different growing conditions. Selecting the right grass seed mixture ensures that different types of grass will thrive in damp, dry, sunny, or shady areas of your lawn. Don't cut corners on quality — a cheap grass mix will usually give you poor results.

A Quick Walk through the Grasses

The Cool-Climate Grasses

Creeping Bent Grass:

Best for: Golf course greens, lawn bowling.

Appearance: Low; velvety.

Strong Points: Best for uses mentioned; not for average lawns.

Weak Points: Must be cut very low or it mats up and develops thatch; susceptible to disease.

May crowd out other lawn varieties and is often treated like a weed; shallow-rooted, so it requires moisture and fertilizer, which also encourages disease.

Mowing: ¼" to 1".

Favorite Varieties: Pencross, started from seed.

Worth Noting: Colonial bent grass is sometimes found in cool, moist, coastal areas, where it can be mixed with fine fescues. It requires a lot of maintenance and is cut longer, from ¾" to 1".

Kentucky Bluegrass:

Best for: Sunny lawns in Zones 1 and 2.

Appearance: Deep green, fine-textured, attractive.

Strong Points: Spreads well; forms strong sod; easy to grow; inexpensive; many varieties to choose from.

Weak Points: Suffers in summer heat and may go dormant or die in extreme conditions. Improved varieties require more maintenance. Most varieties do not do well in shade.

Mowing: 2" to 4" (cut long during summer heat).

Favorite Varieties: With more than 80 varieties to choose from — each with varying characteristics of disease resistance, shade tolerance, drought tolerance, etc. — it is worth having a chat with a local nursery or the Cooperative Extension Service at your state university to determine what kinds of problems are common in your area and which variety they might recommend.

Worth Noting: Rough bluegrass likes wet, shady areas. Varieties are Sabre and Colt. It is shallow-rooted, does not tolerate drought, and may contaminate bluegrass and perennial ryegrass in sunny areas.

Fescues

There are several types of fine-bladed, shade-tolerant grasses in the fescue family, plus some coarse-bladed, tall fescues. These tall fescues have evolved from weed, to forage grass, and finally to a turf grass for areas too warm for the cool-weather grasses. The fine fescues are tough and are often used to overseed poor lawns.

Chewings Fescue:

Best for: Mixes with Kentucky bluegrass because of its tolerance for shade, although it can compete with bluegrass in a lawn.

Strong Points: Tolerates close mowing in cool climates; fine, upright blades; can tolerate traffic; does not require much fertilizer.

Weak Points: Susceptible to disease in areas with warm, moist summers; might clump.

Mowing: 1½" to 2".

Favorite Varieties: Shadow, Cascade.

Creeping Fescue, Red Fescue:

Best for: Even better than chewings fescue in blends with bluegrass.

Strong Points: Fine texture; deep green color; grows well in shade and in dry and acid soils. Once established, it can be left unmowed to create a "meadow" look in naturalized areas.

Weak Points: Susceptible to diseases in hot, moist areas with fertile soils; prefers dry to wet conditions.

Mowing: 1½" to 2½".

Favorite Varieties: Dawson, Flyer, Fortress, Pennlawn, Ensylva, Ruby. Fescues have been improved substantially through breeding since the 1960s.

Worth Noting: They are neither red nor creep. They spread by rhizomes.

Hard Fescue:

Best for: Compared to red fescue, this grass does better in areas with warmer temperatures.

Strong Points: Tolerates shade, dry conditions, and is more disease-resistant than other fescues; low fertilizer requirements; good on poor soils.

Weak Points: Slower to get established.

Mowing: 1" to 2½".

Favorite Varieties: Aurora, Reliant, Tournament, and Waldina are improved varieties.

Worth Noting: A bunch grass; it doesn't spread.

Tall Fescue:

Best for: Play lawns; high-traffic areas.

Strong Points: Green all year long, weather permitting; good in north-south transition areas; good shade tolerance; good in dry conditions if it gets periodic deep waterings.

Weak Points: Medium to coarse texture; might clump; does not mix well with other blends unless it dominates (90 percent or more).

Favorite Varieties: Apache, Clemfine, Rebel, Houndog, Falcon, Mustang. Make sure you have a turf-type tall fescue. These have been improved from the weed and forage crop tall fescues.

Annual (Italian) Ryegrass:

Best for: In a mix, as a nurse grass for better cultivars, because it establishes quickly to provide shade and soil stability; can be useful as a cover crop for vegetable gardens since it grows for one season, then dies.

Strong Points: Few; not for permanent lawns.

Weak Points: Does not mow clean or tolerate cold and heat.

Perennial Ryegrass (Turf Type):

Best for: Playing fields; but not in the far North.

Strong Points: Establishes quickly; blends with bluegrass; new varieties are insect-resistant.

Weak Points: Winter-kills where very cold.

Mowing: 1" to 2".

Favorite Varieties: All Star, Omega (in the North), Manhattan II (for play lawns and fields), Repell, Pennant (low-growing), Citation II, Prelude.

The Warm-Climate Grasses

Bahia Grass:

Best for: Lawns where fine grasses are not necessary or possible; coastal areas; erosion control; sandy soils.

Strong Points: Thick root network helps control erosion; good drought resistance, but does best with frequent rains; wears well.

Weak Points: Considered a weed in finer lawns; forms a coarse, open lawn; needs frequent mowing to look attractive; mole crickets a frequent problem; not easy to mow.

Mowing: 2" to 3".

Favorite Varieties: Argentine, Pensacola.

Worth Noting: Spreads slowly but aggressively through rhizomes.

Bermuda Grass:

Best for: Lawns throughout most of the South; the main grass type of southern lawns.

Strong Points: Easy to grow; likes heat; makes an acceptable lawn with little care; a good lawn when well fertilized and maintained.

Weak Points: Poor shade tolerance; turns brown off-season; invades other plantings.

Mowing: ¾" to 1½".

Favorite Varieties: U–3, Guymon, Numex S–1.

Worth Noting: Spreads by both stolons and rhizomes; common Bermuda grass is planted from seed, while improved varieties are planted from sprigs.

Hybrid or Improved Bermuda Grass:

Best for: Softer, denser, finer-textured lawns wherever Bermuda grass dominates.

Strong Points: More attractive; may stay green longer.

Weak Points: Not for shade; requires more care (water, fertilizer, mowing) than common Bermuda grass; thatch a problem.

Mowing: ½" to 1", frequently.

Favorite Varieties: Sunturf, Tifway, Tiflawn.

Worth Noting: Improved Bermuda grass does best with a regular maintenance program like that found on a golf course.

Centipede Grass:

Best for: Low-maintenance lawns on poor soils.

Strong Points: Crowds out weeds, needs less mowing; resists chinch bugs & rhizoctonia (a fungal disease).

Weak Points: Coarse texture; light green color; may yellow; sensitive to low temperatures; may develop thatch with nitrogen fertilizer use.

Mowing: 1" to 2".

Favorite Varieties: Centiseed (from seed), Oaklawn, Centennial, Raleigh (cool areas).

Worth Noting: Can be used as an alternative to St. Augustine grass; spreads rapidly through stolons, which give it its name; planted by seed, sprigs, or sod.

St. Augustine Grass:

Best for: Shady areas; salty (neutral to alkaline) soils of coastal areas.

Strong Points: Grows fast; tolerates shade and salt.

Weak Points: Coarse; chinch bugs may damage; creates thatch; susceptible to St. Augustine grass virus.

Mowing: 2" to 3".

Favorite Varieties: Roselawn, Better Blue, Floratine.

Zoysia Grass:

Best for: Dense, fine-textured, and somewhat wiry lawns throughout the South and well into the North.

Strong Points: Tolerates heat and drought; resists insects and disease; fine-textured; wears well; dense and resists weeds.

Weak Points: Very slow to establish itself; where summers are short and cool, it has a long period of dormancy when it turns straw-colored; will thatch if overfertilized.

Mowing: 1" to 2". May be hard to mow if it gets long.

Favorite Varieties: There are three species:

- *Zoysia japonica,* which is coarse and winter-hardy. Meyer is a favorite cultivar.

- *Zoysia matrella,* or Manila grass, is coarse, winter-hardy, and tolerates shade. (Flawn for the Mid-Atlantic, Midwestern for cooler climates.)

- *Zoysia tenuifolia,* or Mascarene grass, is the finest-textured and least winter-hardy of the three; okay for southern California.

Emerald is a hybrid that has done well in the southern U.S.; it is dense, dark green, and fine-bladed.

Worth Noting: Although not quite the miracle grass claimed in its early advertising, zoysia does have its positive points. It is planted from plugs of sod that may take from two to three years to spread into a lawn.

Northern Native Grasses

Native grasses may be the best alternative for homeowners who live in difficult areas like the high, dry Great Plains or the shifting sand dunes of coastal areas. These grasses fit nicely with the current trend toward xeriscaping in areas suffering from prolonged drought. Xeriscaping simply is the practice of using all kinds of native plants — ones that survive and even thrive under the local weather conditions — instead of plant stock not native to the area. These plants are often found in low- or no-maintenance areas like roadsides and beaches.

Fairway Crested Wheatgrass:

Fairway Crested Wheatgrass was imported from Russia and is now found in the northern Great Plains and further west to Oregon and Washington, as well as in western Canada. It withstands extreme temperatures, but prefers cold, dry weather and alkaline soils.

Buffalo Grass:

Buffalo Grass is a fine-textured, grayish green grass of the short-grass prairie and does best south of the Fairway Crested Wheatgrass region. It grows and greens during the hot summer and goes dormant in cool weather. Its dense sod was used by early plains settlers to build sod homes.

Blue Grama Grass:

Blue Grama Grass is a drought-resistant bunch grass of the Great Plains and likes cool, dry areas, although it turns brown during severe droughts.

American Beachgrass:

American Beachgrass is a tall, tough grass that spreads underground and is useful for stabilizing beaches. It is found along the Great Lakes, and the Pacific Coast, and from Newfoundland to North Carolina. For best results, plant clumps just before it goes dormant and cut stems back to about two feet.

Avoiding the Weeds

A weed is simply a plant growing in the wrong place. One could argue that the field beyond my garden is full of weeds (including goldenrod), but they are all growing exactly where they ought to be — where I want them to be. The milkweed prospers in the high meadow. The marsh grasses stand on wet feet in a low area just as they should. But in a row of beans, a stray carrot becomes a weed.

This is even more subjective when it comes to lawns, where one person's lawn cultivar is another person's invasive weed.

As a youngster I spent a lot of time mowing a lawn that contained a lot of white clover, which I still think makes an attractive country lawn, even though it is treated like a weed today. My only problem with white clover was that about once a summer, running around barefoot, I would step on a bee that was harvesting honey from a clover blossom.

Now you're more likely to suffer from rashes or respiratory ailments because of the products we've used to get rid of the clover.

The one area about which most people agree is that a lawn is no place for the rough, clumping bunch grasses. We've already discussed annual ryegrass. As I suggested before, avoid grass mixtures in which annual rye exceeds 15 to 20 percent of the mix. Cheap, clumping grass seed is often found in cheap grass seed mixes. Here are some other undesirable grasses to watch for and avoid for lawn use purposes:

- ❦ velvet grass
- ❦ orchard grass
- ❦ reed canarygrass
- ❦ timothy
- ❦ annual bluegrass

CHAPTER 5
FERTILIZE
WITH CARE

I'M CONVINCED that more expensive mistakes are made with fertilization than with any other part of lawn care. I've mentioned a few things already that are worth repeating here.

First, if you leave grass clippings to break down on the lawn, up to half of your fertilizer needs may be met already.

Second, unless the chemical balance of your lawn is somewhere around 6.5 pH, nutrients can be "locked up" and not readily available to the plants.

Third, too much fast-acting nitrogen fertilizer along with mowing the grass too short is a sure recipe for a thatch problem.

Fourth, plants absorb fertilizer slowly. Overapplication only means that you've wasted money and perhaps have been responsible for fertilizer run-off, which can cause problems elsewhere.

Fifth, resist the "miracle cures."

Plants may not be able to tell us what they like, but they are able to show us. If they are strong and healthy and stay that way, we know we are doing something right.

The tricky part about lawn fertilization is that an overdose of fast-acting chemical fertilizer can make your grass look strong and healthy — for a while. But then the lawn begins to suffer during dry spells; it develops a case of thatch; or disease, stress, or some other problem turns up. It's a little like the long-distance runner who sprints away from the starting line but has no energy left for the rest of the race.

Like a successful runner, your plants need two strong legs. The healthy soil we have discussed is one leg. The chemical balance of the soil — the pH — is necessary for the plant. A healthy soil has a structure rich in organic matter and the soil life is active. The other leg is the fertilizer blend that is available within the soil. My philosophy is: feed the soil and the soil will feed the plant. The all-out chemical approach tends to be: for quick results, feed the plant. However, this can

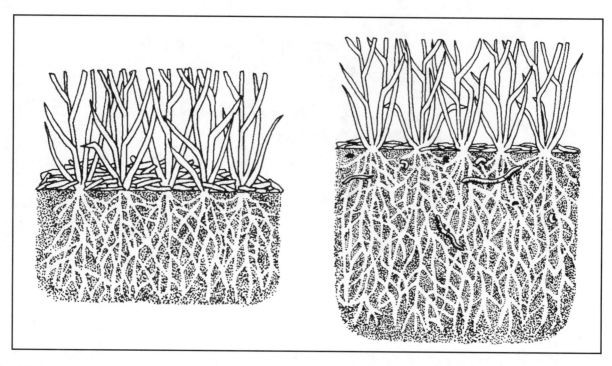

A chemically treated lawn may look lush, until you look at it more closely. Overfertilization can create a layer of thatch (left) that prevents nutrients from reaching the roots and can also damage soil life. But a lawn that is fertilized with organic or bridge fertilizers (right) has an active soil life, which helps break down organic matter, releasing nutrients needed for growth.

sometimes promote fast growth at the expense of the soil life. Be careful about making your plants feel too good too fast with a dose of chemicals, only to have them suffer from a long hangover later on.

Too much fertilizer can result in a plant literally growing itself to death. Since chemical fertilizers are salts, overapplication can also result in fertilizer "burn," which means that the fertilizer actually draws the moisture out of the plant.

A little background information on fertilizers will be a big help when you head down to the garden center for a lawn or garden fertilizer. Lawn and garden fertilizers will have different formulations because the plant requirements are different. Fertilizers all have three magic numbers on them. The most common ones are 5–10–10 or 10–10–10, but you might find some as high as 30–10–10 and others as low as 1–1–1. The high numbers indicate concentrated chemical fertilizers and the low numbers represent the so-called organic fertilizers.

Recently we have seen the development of "bridge" or combination fertilizers, which contain small amounts of chemical fertilizers and large amounts of organic fertilizer. The chemical components provide enough nutrients directly to the plants to produce growth without harming them, while the organic components encourage healthy soil. When the chemicals used in these bridge fertilizers are the slow-release type, the grass will green up a little faster than with regular organics, but the soil life will not be harmed. Even those fertilizers with numbers as high as 15–5–5 can be used if they include slow-release nitrogen (see discussion on page 46).

What do those three numbers on the bag mean? The first number tells you the percentage of nitrogen in a fertilizer. Lawn fertilizers usually have a relatively high first number because nitrogen encourages the growth of foliage and grass is a foliage plant. Nitrogen makes your lawn healthy and green. It is found in proteins and chlorophyll, the pigment that assists in photosynthesis. Plants lacking in nitrogen will grow slowly and older leaves will tend to turn yellow. But too much nitrogen will produce an abundance of foliage at the expense of a healthy root system, which is why overfeeding may produce thatch and a lawn that is shallow-rooted and unable to survive through stress or long dry periods. It also requires more mowing and watering.

The second number gives the percentage of phosphorus. Root crops, including bulbs like tulips and iris, thrive when the second number is high. Phosphorus, though, encourages root development in all plants. Lawns need phosphorus to develop a deep, healthy root system that will carry them through the hot, dry days of summer and help them resist diseases and pests.

The third number is for potassium, which encourages healthy growth, strong stems, and disease resistance. The list of ingredients in the bag or box will also list a filler that might include manures, peanut or cocoa shells, meals made of ground plant or animal products, and so on. So a 100-pound bag of 5–10–10 contains 5 pounds of nitrogen, 10 pounds of phosphorus, and 10 pounds of potassium, or 25 pounds of fertilizer per hundred pounds. The filler, however, may contain materials that help to add organic matter and important secondary nutrients like calcium, magnesium, and sulphur.

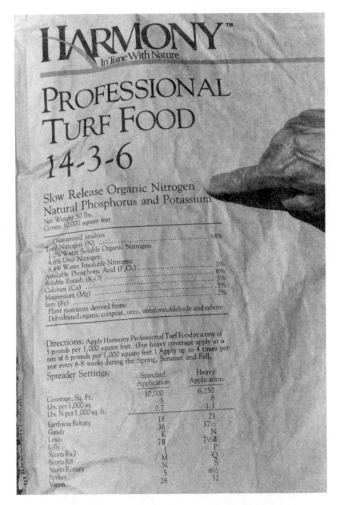

The new "bridge" fertilizers are an ideal way to wean your lawn of its chemical dependency. They feature small amounts of fast-release nitrogen, which helps grass green up quickly, plus slow release nitrogen that supplies nutrients gradually like an organic fertilizer.

Chemical Nitrogen

All nitrogen is not the same, even in a bag of chemical fertilizer. The label may list three types of nitrogen: ammoniacal nitrogen, nitrate nitrogen, and water-insoluble nitrogen. Ammoniacal nitrogen behaves differently from nitrate nitrogen in that it is not usually avail-

NITROGEN-RICH NATURAL FERTILIZERS

Garden centers stock a variety of natural products that are high in nitrogen content. Some of these items are available only regionally. Their approximate N–P–K ratings are as follows:

❦ Bat guano, from 2 to 10 percent (depending on age)–4–1

❦ Blood meal, 12–1–0

❦ Cottonseed meal, 6–2–1

❦ Dry poultry manure, 4–4–2

❦ Alfalfa meal, 3–3–2

❦ Dry sheep manure, 4–1.4–3.5

❦ Soybean meal, 7–10.5–2.3

❦ Feather meal, 11–0–0

❦ Fish meal, 10–4–4

❦ Hoof and horn meal, 12–2–0

❦ Leather meal, 10–0–0

❦ Composted cow manure, 1–1–1

These can all be spread on the surface of the lawn and raked in. Gradually they will be absorbed into the soil and the root zone.

able to the plants until the soil organisms have converted it into nitrate form. This conversion process makes the soil slightly more acidic. Ammoniacal nitrogen does not leach away into the soil as quickly as the nitrate form.

The second type, nitrate nitrogen, is fast-acting but also leaches away quickly. Leaching is an important consideration in fertilizer application. As much as two-thirds of a fertilizer application may leach away before plants are able to make use of it. Not only is this wasted money for you, but the fertilizer can get into waterways, where it encourages the growth of nuisance plants, or into drinking-water supplies. The highly concentrated chemical fertilizers with ratings like 32–10–10 or 20–30–15 are best for houseplants or plants in containers, where water cannot carry the fertilizers away through the soil.

The third kind of nitrogen, water-insoluble, is released slowly and is a good choice for container plants because it can't leach through the soil before it is absorbed.

Some new fertilizers are now available in which the nitrogen is coated and releases very slowly into the soil. These fertilizers can be formulated so that a small percentage of the nitrogen is available immediately to green up the lawn and the balance becomes available gradually, a little like the "time-release" cold medications. As a result, you do not have the high-analysis 32–6–6 kind of fertilizer, but a long-lasting fertilizer in the range of 16–5–5.

Natural Nitrogen

Grass clippings and the grass roots that die in the soil are very important sources of nitrogen for lawns, providing one-half or more of a lawn's fertilizer needs. Many people have successful lawns and never fertilize. Just as the forests survive on their own, so do the grasses. The nitrogen and other nutrients in clippings are returned to the soil as they decompose. It makes no sense to take these to the dump. From time to time the lawn will get ahead of the mowing and large clumps of clippings will be left behind. These can be spread out to dry and then either raked into the lawn or composted.

My "Secret Weapon" Fertilizer

As a vegetable gardener, I made an accidental discovery that changed how I fertilized my gardens. Now I have found that the same thing works for lawns.

One year I was mulching my strawberry beds with straw when I ran out and finished up with some alfalfa hay I had on hand. Later, after the hay had decomposed, I noticed that the plants were much more vigorous and green where the hay had been substituted for the straw. So I began testing alfalfa meal, which is just chopped alfalfa hay, as a fertilizer. I was amazed at the results! Alfalfa is not only rich in nitrogen, but it is also very deep-rooted. Alfalfa roots may penetrate 30 feet or more into the soil. I believe the roots pick up essential trace nutrients from this deep subsoil, and perhaps even pick up some things we haven't analyzed yet that help encourage plant growth. As recently as the 1970s, studies at Michigan State University isolated a growth stimulant in alfalfa called triacontanol that encourages vegetable plants to produce 10 to 15 percent more vegetables.

I began experimenting with alfalfa meal on my lawn and on the golf greens I have been constructing, and have had excellent results.

Some organic fertilizers contain alfalfa meal and those are the ones I look for.

The only drawback for the average homeowner is the fact that alfalfa meal is not available at most garden centers. Alfalfa is more often used as food for animals. Some rabbit food is pelletized alfalfa meal, and so is the kitty litter brand called Litter Green. Living in the country, I go to our local feed store and order 50-pound bags, which cost just a few dollars. Stores that cater to horse owners may also know of a supply of alfalfa meal.

Phosphorus

Phosphorus is represented by the second digit on the fertilizer profile. It helps produce strong, healthy root growth, builds disease resistance, and promotes fruit and seed formation, so it is important for vegetable gardens. Plants that lack phosphorus may have stems that turn red even though the foliage is dark green. Old stems show the symptoms first. Phosphorus is required to build a healthy root system in that critical top few inches of soil, and it contributes to seed germination when planting new lawns.

Unlike nitrogen, phosphorus does not leach out of the soil very quickly. It is found in organic matter, rock phosphate, fish meal, and bone meal. I usually keep some bone meal around to mix into the soil when planting root crops in the vegetable garden and to have available when planting fall bulbs. Because it moves through the soil slowly, it should be mixed into the bottom of the hole when planting bulbs.

Potassium or Potash

The third primary fertilizer component is

potassium, or potash, which promotes strong growth and disease resistance. It will help your lawn stand up to wear and tear, and is just about as important as nitrogen for successful lawns. Since it does not leach out as fast as nitrogen, however, not as much is applied. It is found in potassium sulfate, rock sand, and granite dust. It is also found in wood ashes, although the exact proportions vary depending on whether it is hardwood or softwood. Wood ashes also contain phosphorus, and a typical profile is likely to be about 0–2–6. They should be used sparingly on the lawn or garden, bearing in mind that they act like lime and raise the pH of the soil. Unlike lime, however, wood ashes dissolve quickly and cause a rapid change in soil pH. Apply no more than two pounds per 100 square feet per year.

Other Essential Nutrients

If you were to believe fertilizer bags, you might think that plant growth simply depends on the nitrogen–phosphorous–potassium (N–P–K) content. These are important primary fertilizers, to be sure, but research has identified 16 other key elements necessary for plant growth. Some we take for granted, like carbon, hydrogen, and oxygen. But plants also require secondary nutrients like calcium, magnesium, and sulphur, as well as micronutrients such as iron, copper, and manganese.

Ironically, chemical fertilizers that are relatively balanced in their composition, such as 5–10–10 or 10–10–10 or even 32–16–6, are commonly referred to as "complete" fertilizers. However, they are only complete to the extent that they have balanced amounts of the three basic chemicals. A truly complete fertilizer would feed the soil first and provide a slow-release, on-demand blend of primary and secondary nutrients for the plant. Those fertilizers that contain large amounts of organic matter with small amounts of chemicals have more of the secondary nutrients that plants and soil life need.

Organic and Inorganic Fertilizers

Everything is made up of some kind of chemical structure, even the most natural of fertilizers. Technically, organic fertilizers are defined as those that have their origins based in carbon. However, that is a very broad definition.

As a practical matter, the choice is between organics derived from a variety of plant, animal, and mineral sources, and chemicals made in a factory. Natural organic fertilizers have relatively low N–P–K numbers, break down slowly, and are absorbed slowly; in other words, they feed the soil at a rate the plant can easily absorb. If you believe, as I do, that half of your fertilizer needs can be supplied by allowing grass clippings to decompose on the lawn, you can relax a little. Organic or natural fertilizers cost more per pound than chemical fertilizers, work more slowly, and give you more in the form of secondary and trace nutrients. The good news is that you don't need to use them as much or as often as chemical fertilizers. I get seasonal growth spurts with organic fertilizers, but not the kind of growing frenzy that makes you wonder if you can ever put away the lawn mower.

If you have a totally chemical-fertilized lawn right now, you can start shifting to more organic fertilizers to reduce its dependency on high-analysis chemicals. Look for a fertilizer that has nitrogen as its highest component and is combined with manures, meals, or other organic by-products. Alfalfa meal, as I've mentioned, is my favorite. I also believe that, because lawns have an amazing power to absorb chemicals, small amounts of chemical fertilizers and pesticides can be used without feeling guilty about it. Once you have developed healthy and active soil you'll find yourself in a situation where the lawn can recycle chemicals in small to moderate amounts. In other words, you can have a chemical-free lawn and still use chemicals sparingly.

Building soil life is a matter of adding organic fertilizers such as manures or meals made of ground plant or animal products. Organic fertilizers do their work by making energy available when light, temperature, and moisture activate the plants to go into their normal growth cycles. By contrast, large amounts of water-soluble nitrogen fertilizers promote plant growth at the expense of root growth. They can force growth beyond the energy-producing capacity of the root systems, creating foliage that does not decompose quickly enough because soil life has been damaged. Thatch is the common result. You can easily get on the merry-go-round of more fertilizer, more watering, more top growth and mowing, which requires another round of fertilizer.

I suggest you get off that merry-go-round by finding an organic blend that contains a small amount of chemicals. This way you will build up your soil while still providing nourishment to the plants.

When to Fertilize

Timing is very important when you are using chemical fertilizers and much less important when you are using organic fertilizers or the bridge fertilizers that contain slow-release chemicals as well as organics. Northern and southern lawns are a little different in their growing cycles, and that's why timing becomes important.

Northern lawns are a little like squirrels. They begin to store up food in the early fall, and this is when they will make the best use of the fertilizer. The reason is that in the spring, triggered by the spring rains and longer days, the grass goes into a growth cycle and sends up shoots as well as forming stolons or rhizomes. Lawns use up a lot of their energy during this

A whole range of organic fertilizers are available for lawn and garden use. Products like dried blood and bonemeal may cost more, pound for pound, than chemical fertilizers, but you don't need to use them as frequently, and they feed the soil, not the plant.

period and begin to slow down as the weather gets warm. They may become dormant when the weather gets hot, but they come to life again in the fall. Lawns will grow and propagate in the fall, but not as much as in the spring. It is in the fall that they begin to store up energy in the root systems for that spring burst of growth. So fertilize in the fall — September in the far North through mid-October in milder areas — for best results.

Even if you have a healthy lawn you should fertilize at least twice a year in the North. The second time to fertilize northern lawns is in late spring after the initial spring burst starts slowing down, in late May or possibly June in the far North. This becomes more important if you plan to keep the lawn green by watering through the summer instead of letting it go dormant. That's because the lawn has just used up most of its stored energy in the spring growth, and has little left to feed on over the summer.

In the South, where the growing season is long, more watering takes place, and lawns are subjected to heat stress, you may want to fertilize four to six times a year. The wide-bladed southern grasses grow vigorously and put on a lot of top growth compared to the finer northern bluegrasses and fescues. The warm-climate grasses should be fertilized early in spring before they go into their growth period, during the warm days of summer, and again late in the summer as the growth period slows down.

If you are trying to restore a lawn, fertilize earlier and a little more heavily than normal, and be sure not to cut it too short over the summer. Avoid putting strong chemical fertilizers on northern lawns during the summer dormant period or you may find yourself feeding a healthy crop of summer weeds.

How Much Fertilizer to Apply

Before you get out the sprayer or spreader, think back a moment to the chapter on soil. Did you skip right past that? Well, there are some important things to know about the relationship between the soil and fertilizer.

First, unless the pH of your soil is in the proper range, most of your fertilizer will be unavailable to the plants and wasted. Second, if you had done a complete soil test, you would have a clear idea of just what your soil needs. And third, are you feeding the soil or just the plants with your fertilizer?

If you live in the part of the country with acid soils, which is most of the United States east of the Mississippi, your best fertilizer might be lime (to raise the soil pH), not nitrogen. In the West, your best fertilizer might be sulphur, to lower pH. Nutrients can be locked up in soils that are too acidic (below about 5.5 pH) or too alkaline (above 8.5). In the range between 5.5 and 8.5 you will find the preferred pH of the grasses you want to grow: fescues about 6.5 and bluegrass, ryegrass, and Bermuda grass about 7.5. And pound for pound, limestone is a lot cheaper than most fertilizers.

Unless you like the idea of spending money on fertilizer, bringing it home, and throwing it in the garbage can, find out what your soil pH is and then work toward bringing it into the 6.5 to 7.5 range. Your lawn, your vegetable garden, and your flowers will all grow better. The only exceptions to this rule are the acid-loving plants like azaleas, evergreens, blueberries, violets, and others that your garden center manager can tell you about.

The rule of thumb for fertilizing lawns is to add one-half to one pound of nitrogen per feeding to every 1,000 square feet of lawn. If you're using a chemical fertilizer and spread-ing it with a spreader, you simply have to set it according to the directions.

If you are using organic fertilizers and re-storing a lawn that is in sad shape, you could double or even triple that rule-of-thumb amount on the first application. Every year, more and more organic fertilizers (Harmony, Ringer, Milorganite, Nitron, Fertrel, etc.) reach the marketplace and come packaged with application instructions. However, if you can find my "secret weapon" fertilizer of alfalfa meal, you won't find any directions on the bag. Apply it at the rate of about 10 pounds per 1,000 square feet. This is also the rate at which to apply blood meal.

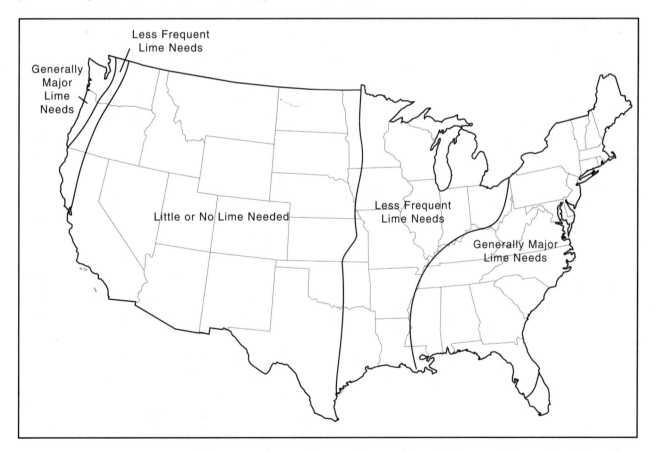

Lawns in the eastern United States and the Pacific Northwest generally have acidic soil and benefit from regular applications of lime. Testing your soil's pH will indicate whether, and how often, you should be spreading lime.

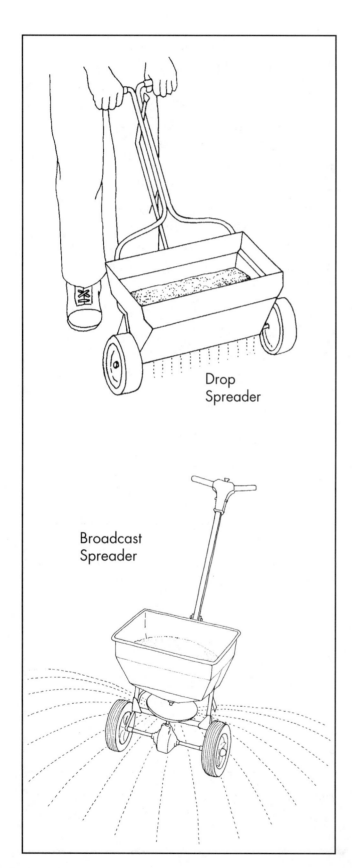

Drop
Spreader

Broadcast
Spreader

Spread, Spray, and Sprinkle

If you are using an organic fertilizer, you will probably be applying it with a spreader. There are two basic types: broadcast spreaders and drop spreaders. Broadcast spreaders send the material into a broad area by dropping the material onto a spinning wheel that then shoots it outward. These are faster than drop spreaders but not as accurate. If you are using a broadcast spreader, try it out to see just how far it shoots material. An asphalt driveway makes a good test area. When actually applying fertilizer, overlap each pass by one-third for an even distribution. Read the directions carefully, and never apply more fertilizer than the bag or box directs.

There are only a couple of tricks to using a spreader. One is to load it off the lawn, particularly when you are applying chemicals. This will help to avoid clumps that can badly burn your lawn. You'll also want to avoid overfertilizing around the edges while you're making your turns. Simply go around the edges first and outline the lawn. I usually take an extra pass around trees and shrubs, because they compete with the lawn for fertilizers. Turn the spreader off as you get near the edge and turn it on when you've made your turn. Keep up the same pace while walking, and remember to shut off the fertilizer flow before slowing down or stopping on the lawn.

Drop spreaders have adjustable settings and are more accurate than broadcast spreaders. Fertilizers often come with settings specified for drop spreaders. They are the best choice for small- to medium-sized lawns. Don't overlap when spreading or growth may become uneven or, with chemicals, you could burn the lawn. Give spreaders a good washing after you use them, because corrosion is one of the few things that can go wrong with them.

There are also two kinds of sprayers: hose-end sprayers and tank sprayers. The organic fertilizers applied in this way could include fish emulsion or seaweed concentrates. Many chemical fertilizers, pesticides, and herbicides are also applied with sprayers. If you are using pesticides or herbicides, be careful what you hit. Herbicides might knock out flowers or vegetables. And never stand downwind from the spray on a breezy day.

Tank sprayers are the more accurate type of sprayer because you pre-mix the ingredients in the right proportions. However, far more people use the less expensive and readily available hose-end sprayers. These are less accurate because they rely on chemicals in the spray container to be siphoned up and mixed with the water passing through the head. If you do decide to use a hose-end sprayer, get one that is big enough for the job or you'll spend a lot of time refilling it. Make sure it is clean and clear, and follow directions carefully. Keep an eye on the level of the fluid in the container or you might end up just spraying water.

I think it's difficult to be accurate with sprayers. Be sure to read and follow the directions carefully and don't apply too much spray, or you could harm your lawn and other plants.

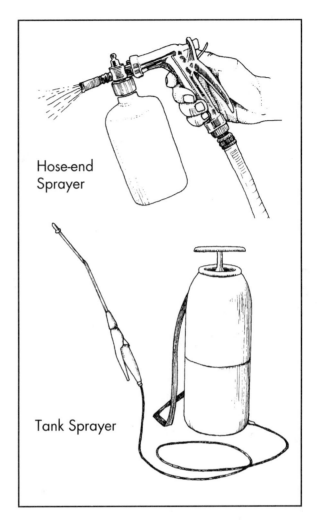

Hose-end Sprayer

Tank Sprayer

CHAPTER 6

WHAT ABOUT WEEDS?

I DON'T SPEND a lot of time worrying about weeds. My feeling is, the best defense is a good offense. A thick, healthy, turf grass lawn won't allow many weeds to take hold. I've noticed that most weeds are found where the lawn is thin. Also, I'm fairly broad-minded about what constitutes a "weed."

Everyone who grows a lawn, no matter where, will have some weeds on it. There's no way to get away from them totally, even if you use herbicides. Herbicides are a temporary solution, but weed seeds continue to travel across the land in dozens of ways, ranging from the wind-borne parachutes of the dandelion to the Velcro-like cocklebur. In fact, the inventor of Velcro studied the cockleburs clinging to his wool trousers and then developed a product based on the same idea.

Weeds are nature's survivors. Some species of pigweed can produce up to 100,000 seeds per plant. Other common weeds, like purslane, not only produce seeds, but also reproduce from leaves and stems that have been chopped up

and left to dry for two weeks. Sometimes these same characteristics prove useful to the lawn owner. Bermuda grass rootstocks can be cut off, dried out, and still spring back to life.

It is our own human nature that defines a weed. Both morning-glories and black-eyed Susans are weeds, but they have flowers that appeal to us, so we cultivate them. Often, weeds are the only plants that will grow in and stabilize poor soils, preventing wind or water erosion.

On the other hand, American agriculture spends more than five billion dollars a year to control weeds, and consumers pick up that cost in food and other agricultural products. Also, there are nuisance aquatic weeds that choke waterways, and some weeds trigger our allergies or cause rashes if we brush against them.

A Healthy Lawn Is the Best Defense

A strong, healthy lawn is the best defense against an invasion of weeds. The lawn will

Broad-leaved weeds like plantain can usually be controlled without spot-spraying with a chemical herbicide. To get rid of a few plants at a time, invest in a dandelion fork or weed popper.

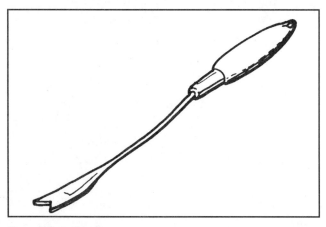

Dandelion Fork

proper mowing, adequate fertilization, and regular watering. So maintenance is the first line of defense against weeds.

In the North it is very common to see cool-climate grasses go dormant during the summer heat, while deep-rooted weeds shoot up and go to seed almost overnight, breeding another crop right on the lawn. High, frequent mowings can prevent them from spreading.

To win the war, I think it helps to understand the enemy, so here are a few basic facts about weeds.

Weeds can be either narrow-leaved, like the grasses, or broad-leaved like the dandelion and plantain that we find in our lawns. Chemical herbicides are often selected for their ability to kill broad-leaved weeds without harming grasses, but they may not be able to distinguish between weeds and broad-leaved flowers and vegetables.

Weeds are either perennials (come back year after year) or annuals (die after the first year). Both usually do a good job of reseeding their immediate area if they are allowed to go to seed.

There are several options available to beat back the weeds.

First, you must decide where you draw the line on weeds. That is, which weeds can you live with and which ones must go? In the North, dandelions are a common problem. Some people wage war on them with a dose of broad-leaved weed killer in the spring, but I look at them as a bright spring flower, knowing that after they blossom they will vanish

shade the ground and provide a canopy of protection against weeds, much as a dense forest canopy discourages growth on the forest floor. In our lawns, where there is a bare spot or an area that is thin, weeds can establish themselves because seeds and roots can reach the ground and take hold without competition. A healthy lawn is the product of healthy soil,

into the spring lawn growth. I enjoy watching the wild rabbits mow them down. Rabbits will bite the stem off close to the ground, eat it, and then just pop the head off and leave it. From time to time I will dig out a particularly large dandelion, but basically my approach is to mow the lawn frequently during dandelion season so they don't get to go to seed. Perhaps the biggest risk in this approach is public opinion. Anti-dandelion neighbors may blame you for every dandelion that appears in their lawn.

Another example is white clover, which is very common on old lawns. Someone who developed a control for white clover declared it a weed, but I mix white clover seed into my lawn mix because I like the low, white blossoms. Because it is a legume, clover fixes nitrogen in its root system and helps feed the lawn its most basic need. Clover is also dense and helps prevent other weeds from getting established. So I put clover on my golf course fairways to reduce the need for fertilizing such a large area.

Second, digging out weeds by hand is an option, but quite frankly it is like trying to stop the tide with a dam of sand. However, it may be workable on a small lawn. A friend of mine rounds up the younger neighborhood children in spring and pays a few cents bounty for each complete dandelion root they bring in. The kids tend to lose interest, though, as soon as they acquire enough for a snack, and in today's world many children don't have to do such lowly work to get what they want. With the current concern about chemical herbicides, new weed-popping tools are showing up on the market, but as yet there has been no easy way invented to eliminate weeds mechanically.

Third, your mowing height and frequency can make a big difference. Cutting the lawn

Get Even with Your Dandelions. Eat Them.

One person's weed is another's dinner. I have an Italian friend who goes looking for young dandelions every spring and puts them in salads. If you are not using chemicals on your lawn, you might want to try using young, tender dandelion blades in a mixed green salad. Dig out the entire taproot with a long-bladed knife or the forked tool made for the purpose. A dandelion is easy to handle if you cut it off again below the crown so the leaves stay together. Use the young, tender leaves either as cooked greens or raw in salad. Harvest them before the plant flowers, since it becomes tough and bitter after flowering.

Sorrel and winter cress are two of the many other edible wild greens that sometimes can be found growing as weeds in a lawn. Back in the days before year-round lettuce, our ancestors relished these tender greens as a welcome "spring tonic," and they still add interest to a green salad. Learning about the edible weeds in your backyard is a lot of fun, and eating them can be sweet revenge.

too short encourages weed growth by eliminating the shade that prevents seeds from getting started. The grasses in your lawn that you consider weeds will blend in better with frequent, but not short, mowing. Weeds grow and set seeds very quickly, depositing thousands of seeds that have the potential to take root. You can't do much about those that come from beyond your lawn, but frequent mowing will prevent massive reseeding on the spot. Don't cut more than one-third of the grass blade's length when mowing.

Fourth, overseed bare ground or thin areas without delay. Bare ground is like an invitation to weeds to overrun the area and then continue to spread. A hay field, turned over and left unplanted, will turn into the most weed-choked field imaginable in only one season. It is a battleground for survival, with weeds quickly taking over, almost as if they knew that unless they become established fast it will be too late. Soon trees will begin to grow and deprive them of sunshine and nutrients.

The vegetable gardener knows this lesson all too well, which is why I suggest turning over garden soil immediately before planting to expose and kill weed seeds that are about to germinate. Lawn renovation is discussed in another section of this book, but if you have a small problem area, you might just break the surface of the ground and stir in some grass seed, or scatter grass seed on thin areas, then rake and water it to encourage the seeds to drop to soil level. Don't wait for spring!

Fifth, you can resort to chemical herbicides. I have pointed out already a lawn's amazing ability to act as a collector and filter, but I still can go only as far as to suggest using herbicides as a last resort, with great care, and on as small an area as necessary.

About Herbicides

Herbicides poison plants, but they do not correct the conditions that caused them to take hold in the first place. Some weeds thrive on acid, dry, or shady soil, where certain types of grass do not grow well. Again, here is where a healthy soil and lawn and a sound maintenance program take over. Correct the problem areas and establish a healthy lawn.

Herbicides may also work against your efforts to build a healthy soil by slowing down the organisms at work within it.

Herbicides do break down in the soil, but in many cases not fast enough to prevent humans exposed to them from developing toxic symptoms. Some commercial firms place printed warnings or plastic ribbon barriers around lawns after applying pesticides, but I have yet to see a dog or a preschooler who can read. Not long ago, I was told about a lawsuit that claimed a dog was poisoned by running onto a newly sprayed lawn. Different herbicides are used for different tasks; however, nonselective herbicides kill any and all vegetation. These are sometimes used on areas like brick patios or gravel driveways to knock out weeds and grasses.

Herbicides are categorized as *pre-emergent* or *post-emergent*, depending on whether you apply them before the target vegetation appears or after it has appeared. The pre-emergent products are applied before the plant appears, forming a film over the soil, and kill the plant as it germinates, long before it appears above the surface of the soil. The common chemical ingredients are atrazine, benefin, bensulide, DCPA, oxadiazon, pendimenthalin, and siduron. Each has specific characteristics that dictate its uses and limitations.

The post-emergent products are applied directly to the plants after they emerge and are often used to kill broadleaf weeds. This can be done either by spraying large areas with a hose-end attachment or by directing a spray bottle at a single plant. Some are sold as granular herbicides and/or mixed with fertilizer. The principal post-emergent chemicals are cacodylic acid, CAMA, MAMA, and MSMA (organic arsenicals), dalapon, dicamba (kills clover), glyphosate, MCPP, 2,4–D, and 2,4–DP. 2,4–D is found in approximately 1,500 products and is suspected of being a carcinogen.

Most, but not all, herbicides currently sold are called *systemic*. That is, they are absorbed by the plant, causing it to die. Some, like poison ivy sprays, are carried in a foam that allows you to see what you've hit. Contact herbicides kill only what they hit.

Although post-emergent herbicides are supposed to benefit lawns by eliminating weeds, a lawn that is under stress may actually be damaged or killed by the herbicide.

If you choose to apply herbicides, follow the directions carefully. Homeowners usually overdo it, figuring that if some is good, more is better. This assumption is simply not true. Whether you're using a spray or a granular herbicide, it is best not to apply it before rain is expected, since its effectiveness is hampered. Dry lawns are best for sprays. Wet lawns are best for applying granules.

Most toxic symptoms blamed on pesticides or herbicides are found in persons who have had direct contact, like walking on a newly treated lawn with bare feet or inhaling sprays.

Common Weeds

Weed identification should be no problem at all, even if you don't know the culprit by name. Simply dig out a sample and find help at your local garden center or state university Cooperative Extension Service. Here are some of the most common weeds.

Grassy Weeds

Annual Bluegrass

It is found wherever Kentucky bluegrass grows. Because it likes cool, moist conditions, it shows up in spring and fall and dies back in the heat of summer, leaving an opportunity for other weeds to establish themselves. Although it's referred to as a winter annual in the South, it can also be a perennial. It must be dug out and then reseeded. Several pre-emergent chemicals can be used, but repeated applications may be necessary.

Bermuda Grass, Devil Grass

In many areas, Bermuda grass is used exclusively for lawns. But, if your lawn is predominantly another type of grass, Bermuda grass is a perennial weed that grows best during the heat of summer and turns brown in the fall. It is most troublesome in transition areas where cool-climate grasses are preferred. Pull and dig it out, making sure you take the roots. Chemicals offer no selective way of knocking it out, but you can spot-treat it with a post-emergent chemical. Avoid watering it in the fall — that just encourages it.

Crabgrass

Crabgrass sprawls its hairy leaves flat along the ground in all directions like a crab's legs, and sends up a shoot to form seeds in late summer or early fall. It is an annual, so catch it before it goes to seed. Keep your mower blades at a high setting, since crabgrass does best on areas that are closely cut or where grass is thin. High mowing is one of the best controls. A thick, healthy lawn will shade out crabgrass before it germinates late in spring, since it does not like shade. Fertilize your lawn early instead of late to feed your grass and not the crabgrass. Chemically, it is controlled by applying pre-emergents before the seeds germinate, but you may also hit any grass seed you are trying to start. Post-emergents include the organic arsenicals, used when the crabgrass is small and usually repeated a week or 10 days later.

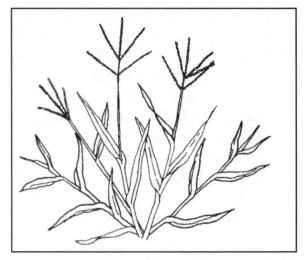

Crabgrass

Creeping Bent grass

Bent grasses are used in golf greens and are a problem when they establish themselves in lawns. Long bent grass will grow horizontally, and you can pick it up in a rake. It is usually cut very short and, when long, it may look brown because only the tips are green. It will thrive if you keep the lawn cut too short. It is shallow-rooted and likes damp areas, so keeping it dry and pointed upward for mowing helps control it. Strong post-emergent, non-selective herbicides may control it.

Dallis Grass

Dallis grass thrives in low, wet areas, and improving the soil situation is the best way to control it. It grows year-round in the South, and may infest Bermuda grass. A perennial with light green leaves, it can be pulled by hand or treated cautiously with post-emergent chemicals — cautiously, because the chemicals may also kill Bahia grass, centipede grass, or St. Augustine grass.

Quack grass

Quack Grass

This is a tough grass to eliminate because of its thick underground rhizomes. It spreads in cool weather. It can be pulled or dug out with some difficulty, or sliced up with a spade and then removed. There are no selective chemical controls, so it is often spot-treated with a post-emergent herbicide.

Wild Garlic, Wild Onion

Wild garlic grows in cool climates. It looks like a clump of grass but isn't. It's easily noticed early in the spring when it gets green before everything else, and it grows well through midsummer. Crush or cut the stems, and they smell like onion or garlic. Control it by close mowing in the spring before everything else is growing. Dig or pull plants before they get large and difficult to control. You may find bulbs, not roots. Chemicals such as 2,4–D are used as a control.

A Last Word on the Grasses

There are many more types of problem grasses than we have listed here, but it is safe to make a few generaliaztions about them. First, there is usually no selective chemical

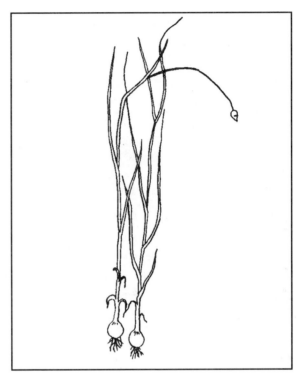

Wild Garlic

treatment, so you are stuck with spot treatment, which should always be done carefully. Non-chemical controls including digging, mowing the grass frequently to prevent reseeding, or leaving it tall to shade out the weeds (the exception is quack grass). It is reasonable to try to control weeds in lawns up to a point, but if more than 40 percent of your lawn has gone over to weeds, your best choice is to dig it out and reseed.

The Broad-Leaved Weeds

Chickweed (annual) and Mouse-Ear Chickweed (perennial)

There are about 150 kinds of these two closely related weeds. Chickweed forms a low, spreading mat with stems that root at the nodes and produces small, white, five-leaved flowers. It prefers shady, moist soils.

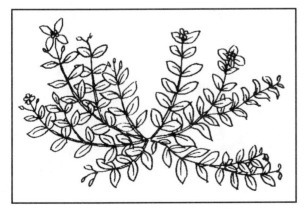

Chickweed

To control chickweed, rake it upright and mow it off, making sure you rake up and remove the runners. It can also be treated with post-emergent chemicals during its spring and fall growth periods.

White Clover

In years past, white clover, with its small blossoms, was valued in lawns, but now it is often viewed as a weed. This is too bad, because as a legume it is a nitrogen producer that provides food for your lawn as it grows, is cut, and decomposes in the soil. It does best on thin soil that has adequate moisture. It can be controlled by pulling or cutting in the spring. Post-emergent chemical controls are used in spring and fall.

Dandelion

This is the most familiar spring invader, with its spreading leaves and bright yellow flower that turns into a parachute-like seed head overnight. A thick, healthy lawn will prevent invasion, but, once established, dandelions can be dug up with simple tools available at garden centers. Invest in a dandelion fork or weed popper.

The best time to dig dandelions is when

Dandelion

their yellow flowers appear and the plant have expended a lot of strength in setting blossoms. Be sure to dig up all of the deep taproot.

Chemicals, often 2,4–D, are applied in spring during the growth spurt but before the yellow flowers appear.

Dock

This name is commonly applied to several weedy plants of the genus *Rumex* — coarse, broad-leaved perennials that grow from one to several feet high. As they mature they produce clusters of flat, scaly flowers on the upper stems. Pop them out or use a post-emergent chemical during their growth season in the spring and fall.

Mallow or Cheeseweed

This annual is called cheeseweed because its seeds look like tiny wheels of cheese. The leaves are roughly circular and they produce a white flower. It can be controlled by pulling it up. Chemical treatment usually involves a post-emergent herbicide applied in mid-spring.

White Clover

Plantain

This common perennial appears in cool seasons and may thrive while bluegrasses go dormant in the heat of summer. There are two main problem species, one with narrow leaves and one with broad leaves, though both are considered broadleaf weeds, not grasses. The seed stem on the broad-leaved plantain resembles a small circular rasp, while the narrow-leaved species has a cluster at the top only. Pollen from plantain bothers hay fever sufferers. You can pull or pop them out. Post-emergent chemical control is applied before the seed spikes form.

Purslane

The fleshy, smooth leaves of this annual (also known as pigweed) may remind you of the indoor jade plant, although they are not as dark a green. You can pull or hoe them off, but the parts seem to spring back to life as soon as you turn your back on them, so clean up after chopping them off and dispose of them carefully. The rose-moss or sunplant is a closely related ornamental species.

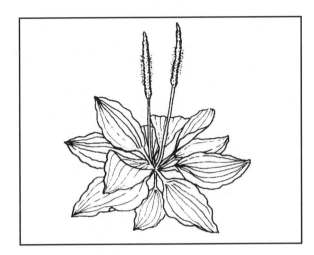

Broad-Leafed Plantain

Purslane spreads by reseeding itself and is found all over the country. It likes hot, dry weather. Chemical control consists of a midsummer application of a post-emergent herbicide like 2,4–D or dicamba.

Canada Thistle

This northern perennial has prickly leaves that sprawl close to the ground. It grows best in the cool weather of spring and fall. Dig it out, or cut and cover it with heavy mulch paper, but be aware that the roots spread underground and that any part of the root can start a new plant.

Canada thistle is the worst of many similar weeds found across the country. Other species of thistle may grow up to six feet tall with flower heads of pink, purple, rose, or white. Goldfinch bird seed is likely to be thistle seed. Mow thistles frequently just before they blossom, or treat them in the fall with a post-emergent chemical. More than one application may be necessary. They can be spot-treated.

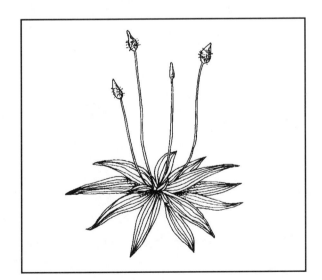

Narrow-Leafed Plantain

Purslane

Veronica or Speedwell

These can be either annual or perennial weeds. They can be tough to kill because they tend to spread below mower height and become very dense. Dig them out completely before they go to seed in the spring. Post-emergent herbicides can be applied when the light blue flowers appear.

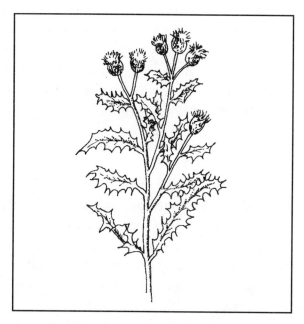

Canadian Thistle

CHAPTER 7

HOW TO DO
THE RIGHT THING FOR YOUR LAWN

I'm a firm believer in not wasting a lot of time and energy doing things that aren't necessary, but I believe just as strongly that if you tackle a job you should do it right, and do it only once. When you are dealing with your lawn and garden, you are also dealing with the natural cycle of things, so timing becomes very important. This timing will vary from one part of the country to another.

So, it becomes a matter of identifying the problem, deciding on the solution, and choosing the right time to do it. That's how we've approached this section of the book — as an A-to-Z guide to techniques and, in some cases, tools needed to do the job. Here's what you'll find, listed alphabetically.

To help you plan your maintenance year, take a look at Chapter 9.

Aeration is the Answer

When the problem with your lawn is compacted soil, the answer is aeration.

Soil can become compacted when people or vehicles compress it, or as the result of thatch buildup. Compacted soil reduces the oxygen supply to the soil life. You'll remember that healthy soil life is essential to help process nutrients and convert them into forms grass can absorb. As soil life declines — often as a result of too much chemical application — the turf loses vigor and weeds can better establish themselves. Often, the overuse of chemicals creates thatch, which again blocks the supply of air, moisture, and fertilizer to the soil. Compacted soils do not absorb water very well. If your soil is compacted, you will find it difficult or impossible to push a screwdriver into the ground up to the handle.

Soil is aerated by poking holes in it, several inches deep, or by pulling out two- to three-inch-deep cores of soil with special equipment.

A simple, down-home method that can work well on small areas is to get a spading fork or similar implement with tines and drive it into the soil, then move it back and forth.

A special, inexpensive tool called a core cultivator is available at most lawn and garden stores. It looks like a giant fork with short tines. The tines are hollow and sharpened. You step the tines into the ground and, as you pull them out, they lift out cores of soil. I leave the cores right on the grass, since they will break down and provide a little top-dress fertilizing. Repeat this process throughout the compacted area.

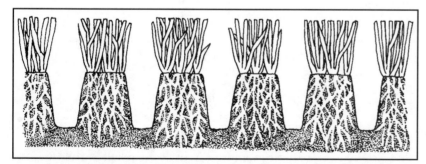

Aerating compacted soil with a core cultivator enables moisture, nutrients, and organic matter to penetrate to the lawn's root.

For larger areas, or when you are doing a complete renovation of a lawn, you can rent an aerator or hire a professional to do the job.

You can aerate any time, but I usually aerate early in the fall, right before the last fertilization, so that some of the fertilizer finds its way into the holes. Be careful if you are using chemical fertilizers. They might burn the roots if they get down into the core holes. Aeration should be done when the soil is moist, but not wet. After I'm finished aerating and fertilizing, I water the lawn.

Aeration is one of the simplest, but most important things you can do to bring a suffocating soil back to life, fight thatch, and prevent weeds from moving in.

Compost: Can't Get Enough of That Wonderful Stuff

Since so many municipal landfills have recently started refusing yard wastes or charging a premium for them, the non-gardening world has discovered composting. That's great news for the environment, and even better news for people who know how to take advantage of compost.

I have been composting for as long as I can remember, and I will guarantee you that, no matter how much yard waste you produce, you can never have enough compost. It is the absolutely perfect thing to put back into your lawn, flower beds, and vegetable garden.

The reason is simple. Compost is loaded with the very soil life — bacteria and beneficial fungi — that the soil needs to make

Making and Using a Simple Wire-Mesh Compost Bin

1. Take a strip of wire mesh three feet wide by nine feet long. This should be heavy mesh (sometimes called turkey wire) with something like a 2 x 4-inch grid. Chicken wire is too flimsy to use without supporting it on stakes pounded into the ground. (To save money, I use chicken wire for big compost bins. If you have a lot of leaves to compost, for example, a chicken wire bin about three to four feet wide and as long as you want could be your best bet.)

2. If you are using turkey wire, just bend it into a circular hoop and wire the ends together. Stand it on end, and you have a compost bin. If you have a lot of material, make a bigger bin or make two bins. Don't make it smaller, because compost piles should not be much less than three feet across and three feet high.

3. Compost needs to be turned to provide oxygen to the soil life and keep it working. Here's how I do it with the small, stiff wire bins: when the bin is filled and it's time to turn it, I step right into it and pull up on the wire, kind of like pulling on my trousers. I set the bin down on bare ground next to the pile, and use a spading fork to turn the pile back into the bin, a chunk at a time.

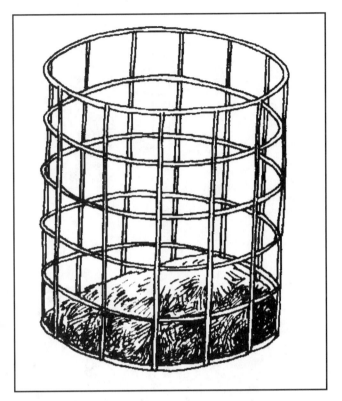

Wire-Mesh Compost Bin

food available to plants. In a compost pile, this hungry soil life turns yard wastes and kitchen scraps into rich brown *humus* — a kind of soil made up completely of organic matter. Add this to the lawn and garden and you can almost see the plants smile. For lawns, you should run it through a screen of half-inch hardware cloth and return the big lumps to the compost pile.

Compost works especially well where soil is sandy, thin, or old and tired. It will help loosen up the soil. Raking compost into an area that has just been aerated will help get it down into the root zone where it can work to build the soil.

A compost pile won't smell or attract pests if properly cared for, it won't require much maintenance — just turning now and then.

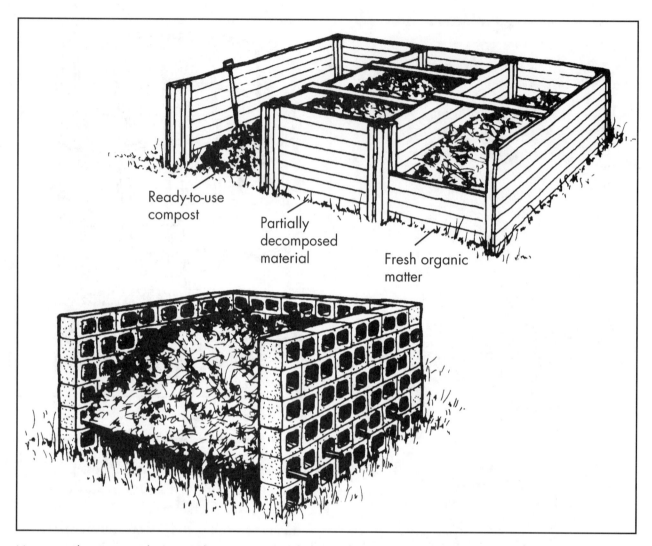

Ready-to-use compost

Partially decomposed material

Fresh organic matter

Homemade compost bins can be constructed from a variety of materials, so long as they are built at least three feet square and allow for proper air circulation in and around the pile. The wooden three-part compost organizer (top) and the cinder block design with perforated plastic tubing (bottom) are only two possible designs.

Since composting has been rediscovered, many compost-making machines have come onto the market, but I stick with a system I've used for years. As you might guess, I produce lots of yard waste from my gardens and property, so I need a system that is inexpensive and simple. For the average home, my system should cost no more than 10 to 20 dollars and will take up only a few square feet in the back corner of the yard.

There are many kinds of homemade compost bins, constructed of free or inexpensive materials: short sections of snow fence might be available free from the city or county road commission; cinder blocks can be stacked with open ends facing the pile to provide air; wooden shipping pallets can be picked up free and made into a three-sided box. Whatever

If you're like me, you'll never have enough compost. No matter how much yard, garden, and kitchen waste I make into compost, I always seem to find another use for my rich, organic "black gold."

you use, just remember you need to be able to somehow get at the compost.

Making Compost

There are two basic ways to make compost. One is to put all the organic material into a bin and forget about it. Gradually it will break down, but this might take anywhere from several months to a year. The second method speeds up the process by giving bacteria and other soil life exactly what they need to transfer organic waste into humus: air, moisture, and an activator. With a little attention, this compost pile will heat up to 140°F (60°C) to kill weed seeds and be ready to use in about a month. Yes, those bacteria get so active the pile will actually get hot. For the same reason, farmers have to be careful when they put green hay into the barn, because this heating process is what causes spontaneous-combustion barn fires.

1. Once your bin is constructed and ready to go, place a two- to six-inch-thick layer of coarse material, like leaves, hay, weeds, or even small twigs, in the bottom.

2. Sprinkle on a large handful of a compost activator that is rich in nitrogen and protein,

Leaves can be gathered up in the fall and composted to make a rich leaf mold, or saved to be added in layers to the compost pile.

thoroughly covering the coarse material. Manure (not pet droppings), rich soil, sod, alfalfa meal, bone meal, blood meal, fish meal, hoof or horn meal, and cottonseed meal are all good choices. Once you have some compost, you can even use it as an activator. Dry dog food will do the trick, too. Do not use chemical fertilizers in a compost pile.

3. Continue building the pile by alternating layers of coarse material and activator. Ideally, your mix would consist of roughly one part of materials high in nitrogen to about 25 parts of materials high in carbon. Materials high in nitrogen generally include leafy or green things like kitchen waste, grass clippings, alfalfa meal, alfalfa hay, and rotten manure. Those high in carbon include things like fallen tree leaves, cornstalks, and straw.

4. Moisten the pile thoroughly, but don't soak it. The center of the pile must remain loose to allow air inside.

5. The pile will heat up in a few days, sometimes within hours.

6. In about a week's time, turn the pile. Try to get the material from the outside into the center. If the pile seems dry, moisten it again. Continue turning the pile about once a week.

Things to Add to Your Compost Pile

Alfalfa meal and alfalfa hay (the meal will activate the pile)

Algae (pond weeds)

Apple pomace (cider press waste)

Ashes (wood, not coal; sprinkle lightly between layers, don't add ashes in big clumps)

Banana skins (as well as all fruit and vegetable peels, stalks, and foliage)

Bean shells and stalks

Bird cage cleanings

Broccoli stalks (shred, cut, or pound soft with a mallet)

Buckwheat hulls or straw

Cabbage stalks and leaves

Cat litter (prophyllite, alfalfa pellets, or vermiculite before the cat has used it).

Citrus wastes and rinds

Clover

Coffee wastes and grounds

Corn cobs (shred or chop)

Cottonseed hulls

Cotton waste (also known as "gin trash")

Cowpeas, pods and vines

Cucumber vines (unless they are diseased or insect-infected)

Dog food (dry food is a nitrogen/protein activator)

Earthworms

Eelgrass

Eggshells (grind or crush)

Fish scraps (bury in the center of the pile)

Flowers

Grape pomace (winery waste)

Granite dust (available in quantity from most rock quarries)

Grass clippings (let dry first and use in thin layers between other materials; a thick mass will be a mess)

Greensand

Hay (mixed grasses or salt marsh hay)

Hedge clippings

Hops (brewery waste)

Kelp (seaweed)

Leaf mold

Leaves

Lettuce

Lime (agricultural)

Limestone (ground)

Milk (sour)

Muck

Melon wastes (vines, leaves, and rinds, unless diseased or infested)

Oat straw

Olive residues

Pea pods and vines

Peanut hulls

Peat moss

Phosphate rock

Pine needles (use sparingly; they are acidic and break down slowly)

Potato wastes (skins, etc.; watch out for insect-infested vines)

Rhubarb leaves

Rice hulls

Shells (ground clam, crab, lobster, mussel, and oyster)

Sod and soil removed from other areas

Soybean straw

Sphagnum moss

Sugar cane residue (bagasse)

Tea leaves

Vetch

Weeds (even with seeds, which will be killed as the pile heats up)

Wheat straw

7. The compost will be ready to use when the pile no longer heats up — in about a month. It will not be uniform and evenly decomposed, but don't worry about that. If you're going to need fine particles for top-dressing, shake the compost through a screen of half-inch hardware cloth. I've made a frame of 2 x 4s with hardware cloth on the bottom that fits over my garden cart. The lumps can either go back into the compost bin or be used in vegetable or flower gardens. Some things, like broccoli stalks, seem to take forever to break down. I give them a head start by smashing them a little with a hammer.

Compost Tips and Tricks

Kitchen Wastes

A covered bucket under the kitchen sink can recycle most of your kitchen wastes including vegetable trimmings, eggshells, sour milk, and coffee grounds. Avoid meat wastes, since they may attract pests. Kitchen wastes are best kept covered and in the center of the compost pile.

Grass Clippings

Most of your grass clippings should be left on the lawn to decompose and refertilize the grass, but if you come back from vacation and your lawn looks like a hay field, you may want to get the big clumps of clippings off the grass. Spread them out a few inches thick for a few days to dry, before adding them to the compost pile. A heap of fresh grass clippings will only turn into a smelly mess. Never compost grass clippings from a lawn that has been treated with herbicides or pesticides.

Leaves

Leaves break down very slowly unless they are in a pile that is activated. Sooner or later, though, they will break down.

Questionable Materials

I don't compost newspapers, sawdust, charcoal, weeds that have gone to seed (although a well-managed compost pile will heat up enough to kill weed seeds), sludge from human waste, and things that don't decompose. Wood ashes can be added in small quantities — not more than one gallon to a three-foot pile.

Mowing Makes the Most Difference

Mow higher and leave the clippings on the lawn is the best advice I can give you. This can make a big difference in your lawn even if you don't do anything else.

The rule of thumb for mowing is never to cut more than one-third of the growth. There is a very good reason for this. Grass

The two most important tenets of mowing are: never mow more than a third of the grass's height at one time, and leave the clippings on the lawn to fertilize the soil.

plants produce their food in their foliage through the process of photosynthesis. A scalped lawn is starved, and you actually can mow a lawn to death. For example, if you go off on vacation and come back to a lawn that is six inches high, and then cut it way back, you have created a bad situation. The lawn has lost its ability to manufacture food, so it will draw on all the reserves in its root system to put on new foliage. If you have been feeding the lawn chemically, and as a result have created a shallow-rooted lawn, it might just exhaust itself.

In healthy soil, grass clippings will begin to decompose almost immediately and recycle

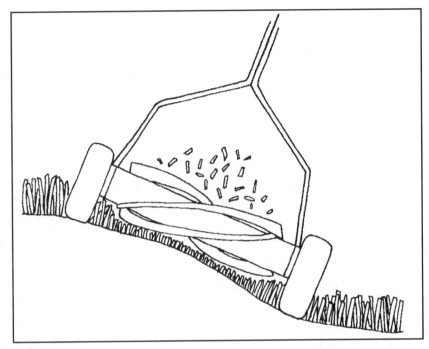

Be careful not to scalp your lawn when mowing the contours of a sloping area. Thin or dying grass on a hillside can easily lead to erosion.

moisture and nitrogen back into the turf. A University of Connecticut study found that the nitrogen from grass clippings showed up in growing grass within two weeks. At the end of three years, the researchers found that about one-third of the nitrogen in the grass came from recycled clippings. So at least a third of the fertilizer your lawn needs is already taken care of when clippings are recycled and, in my experience, it's as much as one half.

You'll notice I said *in healthy soil*. A lawn that has been on a chemical diet may not be based on healthy soil, since chemical lawn treatments can damage the microorganisms that are essential to healthy soil. You can wean your lawn away from chemical dependency by changing to one of the new bridge or organic lawn fertilizers.

I suspect that one of the greatest problems

with lawns is that mowing becomes such a routine that it is easy to lose sight of the fact that, as the seasons change, so does a lawn's needs. A teenager is shanghaied into service before he or she can escape to join friends. Dad rushes through mowing on Saturday morning before heading to the golf course. Mom gets stuck with the job because everyone else has vanished. Or, the lawn service comes once a week on schedule. As a result, the lawn gets cut once a week at whatever height the mower was set to when it was last pushed into the garage.

Grass has a seasonal life cycle, and here's how I mow mine to account for it.

1. Early in the spring I make an inspection and cleanup tour to check for winter damage, for fungi that may have appeared with the retreating snow, and to rake and pick up debris.

2. My first cutting, before the lawn even greens up, is fairly short, about one and one-half inches. This cutting takes place as soon as the lawn dries out in the spring, and it opens up the emerging lawn to air circulation and sunshine. Always wait until the grass is dry before you mow, at any time of the year.

I make the last cutting of the fall fairly short, so my spring mowing is just a bit of a trim. If you have let the lawn go in the fall, you will probably find areas where the grass has been matted down over the winter. Grass needs to be standing up straight when it is cut. If it isn't, brush it upright with a broom rake. Possibly you'll find long, trailing, beardlike patches of grass. This is bent grass. It should be raked upright and given a crew cut.

3. For the next two or three mowings — the period just before the lawn goes into its vigorous spring growth spurt — I set the mower up one-half inch, to about two inches. The lawn is now expanding and spreading. Sometimes, at the beginning of this period, I give it a light fertilization. Usually, I just fertilize areas that seem to be less vigorous than the rest of the lawn.

4. When the grass starts growing rapidly, I raise the mower again. I want to keep it at a three-inch height throughout this growth period to crowd out spring weed seeds. Probably you've been cutting it shorter than this, so it takes a little self-discipline to let it grow out and then keep it there. At this time of the year it sometimes seems that it has grown back before I put the mower away. That means that the mowing schedule has to be adjusted to keep the lawn at the correct height — possibly more often than just every Saturday morning. When you keep the lawn a little on the long side, it will need more frequent mowings to look good. By the way, this spring growth is making use of the fertilizer I put on last fall. That's why the fall fertilization is the most important.

Take a good, hard look at your lawn. It may be longer than usual, but it will still look well cared for if it is even. It should not be allowed to get so long that the grass begins to bend over. On the other hand, it should not be cut so short that after mowing it looks pale or yellowish, instead of rich and green. Sometimes it almost seems that homeowners scalp their lawns during this vigorous growth period because they want to take a break from mowing. Resist the urge to teach your lawn a lesson. Remember the rule: don't cut more than one-third of the growth.

5. In late spring I add an organic or bridge fertilizer. When the hot days of summer come, northern lawns enter a dormant period. Unless they're watered regularly they appear to be dying, but, unless conditions are very unusual, they are not. Even with watering, lawns will go dormant in very hot, dry, sunny periods. Unless you are watering, the lawn won't need much mowing, and the mowing it does get should be high.

6. Where I live, the weather cools off early in September and the grass goes into another growth period. Now the grass is storing energy in its root system, using last spring's fertilization, and preparing for next spring's growth after the coming winter. Because grass makes food with its foliage, the lawn should be kept high during this period. There's no need to set the mower down just yet.

7. As autumn sets in, the growth rate slows and the lawn mower comes out less frequently. After we've had a couple of freezes, I lower the mower to about one and one-half inches. I want the lawn on the short side as we go into winter, to prevent it from matting down and inviting fungi. It will make the spring cleanup much easier.

From time to time, unusual circumstances make it necessary to be a little flexible. For example, a rainy spell might make it impossible to mow for a while and the lawn grows up to six inches. The rule of one-third still applies. Don't cut it back three or four inches in one pass. Instead, raise the mower to its maximum height and bring it down a little at a time. If it really has gotten out of hand you might have to rent a high-cutting mower for the first cut, since most mowers top out at about four inches.

Grass clippings should be small enough to drop back down to the soil. If you are leaving clumps or miniature windrows, like a hay field, run the mower over them again or collect them for composting.

Mowing Southern Grasses

The southern grasses are on a different growth cycle from the northern grasses. They grow during the hot days of midsummer and go dormant and brown in winter. That is why a winter grass like annual rye is overseeded at about the time the warm-climate grasses go dormant. It is a winter green-up that is commonly used on golf courses in the South. As the basic grass comes back, the annual rye dies back or is crowded out.

Except for mowing the winter grass, southerners don't really need to follow the growth cycles with their mowing practices as lawn owners do in the North. These rough southern grasses have more or less standard mowing heights throughout the season. The tallest is St. Augustine grass, which can be kept

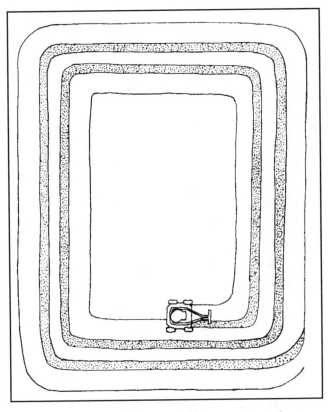

When mowing, overlap your previous pass for a more even cut. When the grass is thick, overlap by half.

at two to three inches, or even taller. Bermuda grass, centipede grass, and zoysia grass do well at one to two inches. Annual rye as a winter grass does well at a height between one and one-half and three inches.

During their growth period in the summer, these southern grasses may need to be cut more than once a week. At the end of the growing season they can be left on the long side to keep out weeds unless a winter grass is to follow. In that case, cut them on the short side before overseeding with the winter grass.

The basic rule of one-third also applies to southern grasses. Grasses are storing food during their summer growth period and need their foliage to stay healthy.

COMMON SENSE AND SAFETY TIPS FOR MOWING

Wet Grass

Mowing wet grass is dangerous because of slippery footing. Grass also clumps up rather than falling back down between the blades to the soil. Avoid mowing wet grass.

Thick Grass

Go slowly. I remember watching a teenaged athlete mow a thick, tall lawn. He jogged through it. When he was done, the lawn looked like waves on a lake because the mower was pushed over the grass before it had a chance to cut.

Steep Hillsides

It is easy to slide a foot right under your mower. Avoid pushing mowers down steep banks. Cut up or across the hill. Better still, plant a ground cover on the slope and forget about mowing it.

Oil and Gas

Don't refuel or add oil with the mower on the lawn. Some might spill and kill the grass. Find a spot on the pavement. Adding chemical fertilizers to spreaders on the lawn can create spills, too, with fertilizer burn the likely result.

Scout Before You Cut

Clear off rocks, sticks, and other objects that are likely to damage your mower or fly off and injure someone. Pipes and metal stakes used by surveyors may be pushed out of the ground by winter freezing. In our part of the country, a fresh crop of rocks pops out of the ground each spring.

Basic Safety Rules

Never fool around with the mower blade without first disconnecting the spark plug. If children use the mower, make sure they are old enough to understand where the mower's hazards are (discharge chutes, under the edges). Kids think they are immortal and will use a power mower barefoot, if left to their own devices.

Mowing Patterns

Alternate your mowing patterns for an even look. Overlap your previous cut, and resist the temptation to run the wheel back over the wheel track you left on the last pass. Overlap more. When the grass is really thick, overlap by half.

Maintenance

Keep the mower blade sharp, or it will tend to shred the grass instead of cutting. This invites disease and slows growth, since the foliage has to mend itself. Keep the underside of the mower clean. A drywall or putty knife works well. Grass buildup will restrict air circulation. Mulching mowers are designed to recirculate air to give the blades a chance to pulverize the grass. Keep discharge chutes clear.

Lawn Mowers

It's hard to imagine a better lawn mower than sheep. They are quiet, do not release carbon dioxide into the atmosphere (although they have been accused of producing methane!), and they recycle clippings directly into fertilizer.

Unfortunately, not everyone is in a position to have a few woollies in the backyard. As a result, new and improved versions of the mechanical lawn mower that was invented back in 1830 are now found in garages around the world.

The Reel Mower

The reel mower is an improved version of the first lawn mower, which was patterned originally after a device used to trim the nap of textiles. Such mowers now are available in push and gasoline-powered versions, and the largest ones are used on golf courses, pulled in gangs behind a tractor. I pushed reel mowers around big lawns in the 1940s and can vouch for the fact that they provide plenty of exercise. Because of this, and for environmental reasons, there is a rebirth of interest in push reel mowers among young homeowners with smaller lawns. The advantage of reel mowers is that they actually cut the grass better than rotary mowers. They snip the grass between two pieces of steel rather than relying on high speed to slash it off.

Reel-type mowers do have a couple of disadvantages, though. When they get dull, special equipment is needed to sharpen them, and that usually means having to take them to a specialist. Also, they work well on fine lawns, but do not have the brute force of a rotary mower when it comes to chopping off tall,

weedy growth and cleaning out overgrown areas. They do not do well on rough terrain, but are able to follow gentle contours very closely. I like to run an old rotary mower around in my vegetable garden after crops like peas and beans are harvested, to chop up the foliage before turning it back into the soil. You wouldn't get very far doing that with a reel mower.

More important, however, is the fact that reel mowers are limited in their height adjustment. It is hard to find a reel mower that will cut higher than two inches, and during the summer and other growth periods, I like to have at least another inch. This is not a big problem in the South; therefore a reel mower

Push-type reel mowers are quiet, clean, provide great exercise, and make a cleaner cut than most rotary mowers.

The newest design in rotary mowers is the mulching mower. It chops grass blades into fine pieces, which decompose quickly on the lawn. Courtesy John Deere & Co.

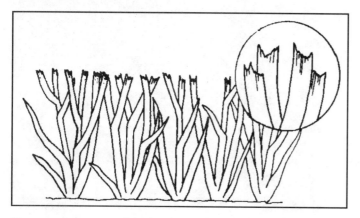

Keep your mower blade sharpened. Dull mower blades tear grass, leaving jagged edges that are unsightly and encourage disease.

might be a good choice if you have Bermuda grass, zoysia grass, or centipede grass. And, if you have bent grass, a reel mower's ability to get close to the ground and follow contours is a definite advantage.

Rotary Power Mowers

Rotary power mowers are by far the most popular models. The general design features a gasoline mower mounted above a housing drive, which encloses a sharp blade that spins like a propeller. The spinning blade actually lifts the grass slightly and helps keep it upright while cutting. The height of the spinning blade is adjusted by raising or lowering the wheels in relationship to the housing. The chopped grass exits the housing through a chute in the top or side.

That basic idea has been refined into lawn care "systems" by the mower industry. You can capture the grass clippings in an attached bag and set them out on the curb in plastic bags to clog up our landfills (bad idea) or compost them (better idea). Better still is the newest star on the mower horizon, the mulching mower. By designing the housing to be a chopping chamber and preventing the clippings from escaping too easily, the clippings are cut and recut and then propelled downward though the grass to the soil. Naturally, this works best if the grass if dry. These mowers will also pulverize autumn leaves to some degree. I like a mower that has the flexibility to mulch (for average summer mowing), blow material back onto the lawn (a light mulch of leaves at the end of the season), and capture clippings and leaves in a bag (for composting).

When buying a mower, it pays to spend a little more to get a commercial or industrial engine. Cheap mowers are no bargain. The housing may crack at its weak points, handles frequently come loose, the motor may fail before its time, and so on. Quality rotary or riding mowers can be a big investment, but don't scrimp. Buy quality and you'll save in the long run.

Rotary mowers are fairly easy to maintain. Most homeowners can sharpen the blades themselves (be sure to remove the spark plug before sticking a hand below the housing). They are fairly trouble-free as long as the air cleaner is kept free of dirt, time is taken to do a proper job of changing the oil (in four-cycle engines), and they are properly winterized. Keeping the inside of the housing clean will improve performance and prevent rust damage. Blades must be kept sharp and free of dents. Dull blades will only shred your foliage. Sharp blades on any kind of mower will help you to create a nice-looking lawn.

If you are debating between purchasing a push version and a self-propelled version, remember that, while it might glide easily across the showroom floor, pushing it though thick grass or up and down hills is quite a different thing. In many families, everybody gets a turn at mowing the lawn. If you buy a mower that only you can manage, guess who gets to mow the lawn every time. Remember, the larger the wheels, the easier it will be to push.

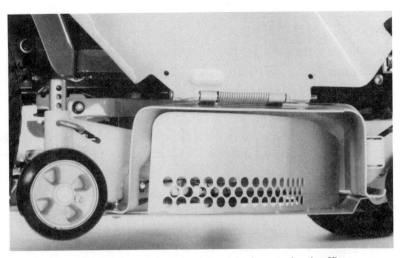

A close-up view of a mulching mower shows the baffles designed to separate the chopped blades of grass and blow them into the lawn as fine clippings.
Courtesy John Deere & Co.

If you have a large-sized lawn, owning a good riding mower can make all the difference in the world. Like me, you may even start to enjoy mowing instead of considering it a never-ending chore.

New rotary mowers are safer than those of the past that did not have the "dead-man's" safety features that disconnect the blade or kill the engine when the handle grip is released.

Even so, make sure that everyone who uses the mower is familiar with all the safety procedures. This is particularly true of children. People don't grow new parts like starfish do.

Repairing Small Sections of Lawn

I take a walk around the property every spring with my notebook to make a "to do" list. I'm always surprised at how many things can cause damaged spots: a gasoline or oil spill, pets, heavy-traffic or play areas, a disease, or insect damage. Or maybe I've just decided to change the landscaping around.

My approach is to keep it as simple as possible, so I handle damaged areas in one of two ways: sodding or reseeding. I have enough space to maintain a small "sod bank," where I can grow a good basic mix and make a withdrawal whenever I need a patch. Good nurseries often stock a small amount of sod for repairs. If you are growing the southern grasses that are started with sprigs or plugs, take a look at Chapter 8 on starting a new lawn. My decision whether to sod or to seed is based on how fast I need results. An area that is going to get traffic soon will get the sod. A bank that might erode before the seed germinates will also get the sod.

Removing Damaged Turf

I don't have many problems with disease or serious insect infestations, but if that's your problem, be sure to inspect the area carefully so you will understand the full extent of the problem. You'll want to dispose of the turf you remove in a way that won't spread the problem.

Removing damaged turf is fairly easy. First, I give the area a good watering to soften it up. Remember to make it moist, but not muddy. For small patches I use a sharp, flat-nosed spade, pushing it straight into the ground to outline the area. Then, slide the spade underneath the sod so you get about an inch or so of the roots. With a little practice you can skin back the sod easily . It curls back on itself as you go, exposing the soil beneath. If you find a lot of white grubs under there, refer to Chapter 11 on insects. Dig out deep-rooted weeds, like dandelions. As long as it's not diseased, whatever comes out can go right onto the compost pile. For larger areas, I use a rototiller and rake up the turf after making several passes. This also aerates the top several inches of soil. You can do the same thing with a sharp-nosed spade.

Once the soil is exposed, you'll have a better chance to improve it in order to get your repair job off to a good start. Possibly it will need to be aerated after having been compacted. If what it needs is organic matter, spread two inches of compost or wet peat moss on the surface and work it into the soil to a depth of about six inches. If you've tested the soil and it needs to be balanced or fertilized, mix in fertilizer, lime, or sulphur as needed. If you have worked peat moss into the soil already, remember that it is slightly acidic and you may need to add lime to compensate.

Then continue with the same seeding practices mentioned above. If you are laying sod, allow for one inch of extra height in preparing the soil. That will account for the thickness of the sod. If you are faced with fixing up a very large area, see Chapter 8 on establishing a new lawn.

REMOVING DAMAGED TURF

2. Push a flat-nosed spade straight into the ground, outlining the area to be removed.

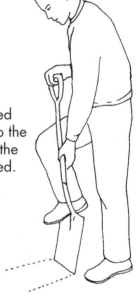

1. Water the damaged area, making it moist but not muddy.

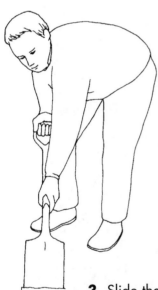

3. Slide the spade underneath the sod, cutting down an inch or so into the roots.

4. Push the spade forward underneath the sod, which will curl back on itself, exposing the soil beneath.

STEP-BY-STEP SPOT SEEDING

If an area of your lawn is thin and needs a boost, you can spot-seed it. Dig or pull up any weeds, and then give the soil a good roughing up with a steel garden rake, or even a vegetable garden cultivator. Take it easy on the grass already growing there. Mix about two-thirds garden soil with one-third peat moss and about one cup of organic or bridge lawn fertilizer per bushel. If you have compost available, run it through a screen to take out the lumps and then mix it in. Work this mixture into the soil as much as you can with the rake, then level it out.

Sometimes the problem is caused by having the wrong kind of seed in a particular area. For example, a shady area may have too much bluegrass and not enough fescue. If that's the case, this is your chance to replant with the right mix. Otherwise, plant the same mix that you have in the surrounding area. If you want to get it off to a fast start to hold the soil in place, make sure there is some annual rye in the mix. It germinates quickly for one season and then dies back, allowing the better seeds to fill in.

Sprinkle on enough seed to cover the area — at least 15 seeds per inch. It doesn't hurt to overseed the surrounding area somewhat. Rake the seed into the bare soil until it's buried about an eighth of an inch deep. Where the lawn is established and you've overseeded, rake it in with a broom rake. Then, tamp the newly seeded area down, or roll it if it is large. Cover the area with mulch, such as straw, or fabric made for lawn-starting, and water it until the water penetrates about six inches into the soil. Keep the area moist, watering it every day if necessary, until the grass is about two inches long. Begin mowing when it reaches about three inches.

1. To prepare a small area of lawn for spot seeding, the first thing to do is rough up the soil using a metal garden rake.

2. Then mix one part peat moss with two parts garden soil. Peat moss is an excellent organic soil conditioner — it lightens up the soil, increasing its water-holding capacity in the crucial time when the germinating grass seeds need moisture. It also helps to premoisten the peat moss; just move the bale outside the night before you plan to seed and punch a small hole in the plastic bag. Then run the end of a hose into the bale and soak the peat.

3. Next, spread the garden soil/peat moss mixture over the seedbed area. If you have some compost available, now is the time to add it (passing it through a screen first to eliminate any large chunks), along with about a cup of an organic or bridge fertilizer for every bushel of soil. Work in the soil amendments and fertilizer thoroughly with your garden rake and level off the top of the seedbed.

4. Sprinkle on enough grass seed to cover the area — at least 15 seeds per square inch. I normally sow some seeds on the ground surrounding the seedbed as well. Using a seed mix that contains about 5 to 10 percent annual ryegrass is a good idea. The rye grows quickly, holding the soil in place and keeping down the weeds. By the time that the ryegrass dies back, the other grasses in the mixture are ready to take over.

5. Rake the seed into the bare soil, covering the seeds about one-eighth of an inch deep. Using a garden rake, as I'm doing here, is fine as long as you're careful and are establishing seeds on bare ground. If you are overseeding an existing area of lawn, use a broom rake instead.

6. Tamp the newly seeded area down gently if it is small. For larger seedbeds, use a roller. The object is to get the seeds in firm contact with the soil so they will germinate readily.

7. Mulch the seeded area with clean straw, or with a man-made landscape cloth used for seed starting. (Don't use regular hay as a mulch; it's bound to contain weed seeds.)

After mulching, water the area until the water penetrates six inches deep into the soil. From now on, you'll have to check the seedbed every day, watering it as needed, until the new grass is two inches long. Begin mowing when the grass is about three inches tall.

Whether you rent or own one, a rototiller is handy for turning under old lawns and gardens and cultivating new seedbeds.

Here I am running a roller over a freshly planted seedbed. It's the quickest and easiest way to ensure that grass seeds or sod are in firm contact with the ground.

Rollers

There are several situations that call for a lawn roller; however, a roller would be near the bottom of my list of items to own. You can rent them easily because most rollers are hollow (which allows you to wrestle them in and out of a station wagon) and are weighted by filling them with water on site. The amount of water you put in can be varied to supply the amount of weight you need.

When to use a roller:

1. In the spring, when the frost has pushed up clumps of grass and you want to even out the lawn.

2. After you have laid down sod, to make sure the root system is in firm contact with the ground.

3. After rototilling, to flatten out soil that has been fluffed up.

4. After spreading seeds and raking them into a new lawn.

5. After sprigging or plugging a new lawn.

Sprayers and Spraying

Sprayers are used for applying herbicides, pesticides, and liquid fertilizers. They are handy for a variety of lawn and garden uses. For example, if you are using organic techniques, you can apply insecticidal soaps, dormant oil spray (on fruit trees), organic pesticides, and some fertilizers. I think sprayers are much better for applying pesticides than fertilizers, since it is very hard to get an even application with a spray.

Most people will own one of three basic types of sprayer:

A small self-contained hand unit

These feature a small reservoir at the end of a cylinder that is pumped. They are designed for spot applications, like hitting individual broad-leaved weeds with a herbicide. Vegetable gardeners often use these to apply their homemade bug remedies. But, unless they are carefully maintained, they plug up easily, and the cheap models can get rusty and fall apart.

The hose-end unit

This is a nozzle with a reservoir that screws onto the end of a hose. I don't like these very much because, no matter how carefully you measure the blend of water and whatever else you are spraying, you inevitably get too much water or — even worse — too much chemical. The only thing for which I really trust these is spraying liquid soaps, where the mixture isn't quite so critical. Some of these sprayers have nozzle adjustments that allow you to shoot a stream to the top of a semi-dwarf fruit tree or even higher. This can be handy if you use insecticidal soaps or want to hit some tent caterpillar nests with Bt (the common name for *Bacillus thuringiensis*, a biological insecticide). Get one with a large enough capacity to do the job. The smallest ones are only good for very small projects. Clean them thoroughly after use.

Backpack or portable sprayers

I use these because it's not practical to run hose all over my property and because they are very accurate. The spray and water are mixed together inside a big, but portable, reservoir, and then pumped up to provide pressure. I think they're great, and most homeowners don't need anything more than one of these to do all their spraying.

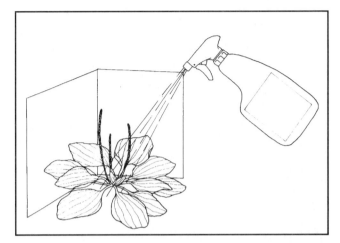

When using a hand sprayer with a chemical herbicide, try to avoid hitting anything more than just the weed that you intend to kill.

Spreaders

Spreaders are very useful, particularly if you plan to follow the maintenance schedule I recommend. The fact is, not having a spreader might cause you to try to avoid the necessary maintenance schedule I have suggested previously. Spreaders are used for:

1. Spreading seed on new lawns.

2. Spreading lime or sulphur to balance the soil.

3. Spreading fertilizer.

Before buying a spreader you should think about what kind of fertilizer you are going to be using. Organic or bridge fertilizers may not be the same size or shape as chemicals, so make sure you will be able to use the spreader with the material you plan to apply. Some fertilizers for instance, are pelletized, not granular.

You have two basic choices:

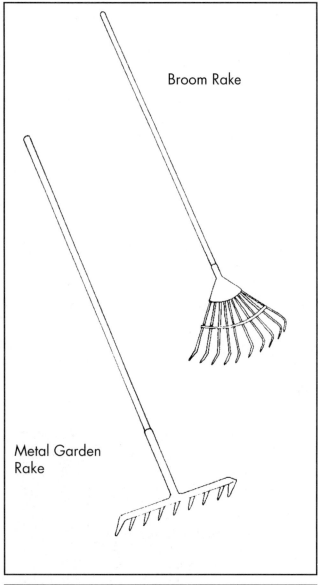

Broom Rake

Metal Garden
Rake

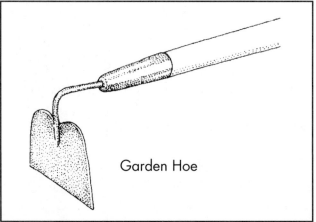

Garden Hoe

Broadcast spreaders

These work by dropping the dry material onto a wheel that spins around and shoots it in a broad pattern. They are the most efficient way to cover large areas. Some are hand-held, and you walk around with them turning a crank. Others are pushed around on two wheels, and the spinning wheel is driven by the rate at which you push. They are not quite as accurate as drop spreaders. If you are spreading herbicides, think ahead about where the material is landing, since it might hit flowers or vegetables. If you want to know how far it throws, try it out on pavement. When you apply fertilizer, go around the edges first and then back and forth across the lawn, overlapping your passes by about one-third.

Drop spreaders

These are fairly accurate and a good choice for most homes. They have adjustable spread rates, and the material is dropped through a gap in a hopper. A paddle-wheel mechanism regulates the flow. Do the edges first, and turn the spreader off as you make your turns. Overlap your wheel marks from pass to pass, but don't double-fertilize or you might have strange green stripes in the lawn later on. You can get an idea about how much fertilizer is being applied by running the spreader over pavement.

Spreaders should never be filled on the grass. Whatever you are applying, too much of it is likely to land where the spreader is placed.

Tools to Make Lawn Care Easier

I have spent more than 50 years with farm, garden, and lawn tools in my hands and I have two very definite opinions: buy strong but not heavy tools, and avoid miracle gadgets.

Lawn mowers and specialty tools have been covered in other parts of this chapter, but a few words on hand tools are necessary. Here are my recommendations for a basic set of hand tools for lawn care.

An iron garden rake

You'll use this for preparing soil for a seedbed and then flip it over to smooth out the soil over the seeds. It will pull out thatch and spread and remove mulch. It is also good for cleaning up. A 15- or 16-inch garden rake is fine. You can find rakes that are built in two ways. One kind has supports coming from both ends of the rake head and then arching back into the handle. This kind of rake will last longer than the second kind, which has a single attachment point in the middle of the rake head.

A broom rake

This is used for cleanup, for brushing top-dressed soil down into the grass, for mixing overseeded grass seed into the surrounding grass, and for other lawn tasks. I have become a real fan of the metal rake that includes a mechanism for adjusting the width of the broom. Its big advantage is its ability to get into tight places. I have also found that it works just fine in the vegetable garden for thinning seedlings.

A flat-nosed spade

Europeans seem to know much more about how to use this tool than Americans. On lawns it can be used to cut out and skin back sod. I use one to make the edges between lawn and flower gardens and also for edging along sidewalks.

A hoe

I use a hoe for eliminating weeds in bare areas. The Reisch hoe has a sharply triangular head.

Weeders

I prefer the old-fashioned asparagus or dandelion fork, which comes with both short and long handles. It is just about the only thing that will remove a dandelion's taproot.

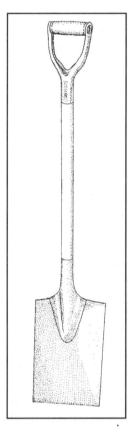

Flat-Nosed Spade

I keep all of my garden tools clean, dry, and well organized in my tool shed. No matter how many hand tools you own, it's always cheaper in the long run to buy sturdy, long-lasting ones and then take good care of them.

A 10 x 10-foot canvas

This is handy for many tasks, from dragging leaves off to the compost pile to piling dirt when you dig a hole for something.

There are a few other tools that I consider essential, but they are not ones that everyone needs. One is a garden cart or wheelbarrow. I use it as much for mixing things as I do for hauling. If you have an old property that you are renovating, you should also have a mattock. This is a chopping tool that is great for breaking apart rotten stumps and digging out old bushes and shrub root systems.

Another tool I like is a lawn sweeper, which you push around like a lawn mower. It sweeps up leaves and grass clippings for composting and can save a lot of time and effort if you have a lot of trees that drop leaves on the lawn.

Watering Equipment and Practices

Get the moisture down into the root zone. That's the best advice I have to offer about watering.

You'll need about an inch of water to penetrate six to eight inches into the soil.

One way to find out if your watering system or sprinkler is doing an even job is to set a bunch of small containers out in the range of your sprinkler and run it until you have enough water in the containers to take a reading. Compare the results at different parts of the sprinkler's range to see if the lawn is getting an even distribution. It will also allow you to calculate how long the sprinkler will need to run in order to dispense one inch of water. You should bear in mind, however, that the time of day a reading is taken will influence how much water gets into the containers. On hot, sunny days you can lose as much as half of your moisture to evaporation. That's why daytime sprinkling is often restricted in drought areas.

I water early in the morning because I like to get up early. I think it's good to have the moisture soak in rather than be lost to evaporation. It also allows time during the day for the leaves to dry out, thus avoiding moisture-loving diseases.

I am tempted to say your lawn needs at least an inch of water a week, but there are always

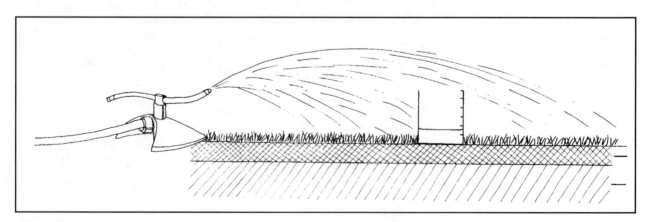

Set up a number of small containers at various distances away from your sprinkler, then see how long it takes to fill them with an inch of water. Use this figure as a benchmark for how long to water your lawn.

exceptions to that rule. You can tell when your lawn really needs water by looking at it closely. If the leaves are rolled or folded over, you have waited a little too long — it is wilting.

No sprinkler system is perfect. For the sake of convenience, it's hard to beat the permanently installed pop-up systems. These can even be put on a timer. The time to install them is when you are putting in a new lawn, after the rough grading has been completed.

I've bought a lot of sprinklers over the years. A vegetable garden's watering needs are different from those of a lawn. I often put oscillating sprinklers up on sawhorses to get the water above tall vegetable plants. That's a trick you can use to expand the reach of your sprinkler.

As for portable sprinklers, I prefer the oscillating type because they water in a fairly straight line along a sidewalk or near a building. They also can be adjusted for spot watering, to put a lot of water into a small area in a short time.

It pays to buy a good hose and take care of it by draining and coiling it before winter's deep freeze. Coiling a cheap plastic hose in cold weather is like wrestling with a python. You can hang it up, turn your back, and it will jump off the rack. Look for a hose made of high-grade rubber and laminated filament. You won't be sorry.

When dry weather sets in, take it easy on the lawn. Don't force growth by feeding it a high-nitrogen fertilizer. Set the mower high, and water it less frequently, but heavily. When you do water, make sure the water is getting down into the root zone. A light watering can be worse than no watering at all, because it

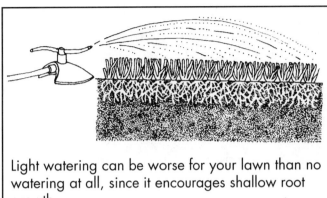

Light watering can be worse for your lawn than no watering at all, since it encourages shallow root growth.

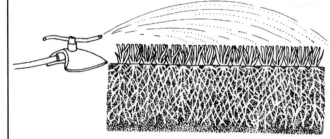

If you water more deeply and less frequently, the roots will go deeper in search of water, becoming stronger, healthier, and more drought-resistant

encourages the roots to reach up, not down, for their water.

How to Spruce Up an Old, Tired Lawn

A variety of problems can bring your lawn to the point at which it needs an overall sprucing up. This is a less drastic step than tearing out a really poor lawn and starting over. I often seed right over existing turf and, at the same time, fix specific problems like thatch buildup or compacted soil. I do this to put new life into areas that are thin, weedy, and do not have the health and vigor that they should. I also use the same method in areas that have been damaged or weakened by insects and disease. The secret, of course, is knowing what the problem really is.

Let's take a little walk around the yard and see what we can learn. I usually take a screwdriver, a notebook, and a trowel along on an inspection tour of the lawn. I might take a magnifying glass along, too, for close-up detective work.

1. How much do I know about the soil in the various parts of the lawn? Is the soil pH what it should be? An application of lime (in the East) or sulphur (in the West), might be the best thing I could do.

2. If there are damaged spots, what caused them? The possibilities include:

❦ Insects (see Chapter 11). Here's where the magnifying glass can come in handy.

❦ Disease (see Chapter 10). Use the magnifying glass again.

❦ Low spots where water stands. This will invite disease.

3. Is there hardpan, ledge, or rock below the soil?

4. Is the soil compacted under play areas or walkways, or where cars pull onto the grass? You should be able to push a screwdriver into the soil up to the handle, without having to pound it with a hammer. Hard soil requires aeration.

5. Thatch. If it is more than one-quarter to one-half inch thick it should be removed, because it is preventing water and fertilizer from penetrating into the root zone.

6. Weeds. Every weed has its season, from the dandelions of spring to the plantain that appears in northern grasses during the heat of summer. If weeds have taken over half of the lawn, think about tearing out the old turf and starting from scratch (see Chapter 8).

7. What has been the fertilization history? Has the grass been fed a steady diet of chemicals that has made it shallow- rooted? Has it been ignored? Were clippings allowed to decompose and feed the turf or were they hauled away? Dig out a plug and look at the root system. A healthy grass plant will have a root mass that is about the same size in bulk, but not in length, as the grass above. Fertilizers may have leached out of high areas into low areas, leaving hilltops thin and low areas rich and green.

8. What has been the mowing practice? Turf cut too short will tend to develop short roots.

Simply changing your routine maintenance practices like mowing and fertilizing will help restore your lawn. Cleaning out thatch, balancing the soil pH, and getting rid of pests will also help to restore it.

Even so, you might want to make an extra effort to spruce up the lawn, at least in troublesome areas, by cleaning it up, improving the soil, and overseeding with new varieties of seed that may do better. You can do this at any time of the year, but I think the early fall is best, about two months before growth stops. Weeds are at the end of their growth cycle and can be removed, giving the new grass seed a chance to get established in the fall without competing with vigorous weed growth.

I test my soil frequently, and find that the early fall is a good time to take a soil test (see Chapter 2) to make sure that all the time and effort I put into improving the soil is going to pay off.

I also consider what grass varieties I will

use to overseed. If it is an old lawn, there are probably improved varieties on the market. Some may resist the types of diseases common to the area. A few even resist insects. Others may be more suited to the local growing conditions. Fescues, for example, will do better in shady areas than bluegrass. If it is a play area in the North, a tall fescue should be considered for its toughness. Some new varieties are low- or slow-growing for reduced maintenance. It is always best to use a mixture of grasses. Those best adapted to the conditions will flourish and fill in for those that do not do well. For specifics on grasses, see Chapter 4.

Preparing the site for overseeding is the first step. In small areas, I use a strong garden rake with iron teeth to remove thatch, pull out weeds, and rough up the surface of the soil. For larger areas, take a trip to the rental store and rent a power rake. They are not very heavy, they are easy to use, and they are very good at removing thatch. You can run the power rake over the area so that weak grass, thatch, and weeds will all come up. With fall overseeding, this raking will pull out a lot of crabgrass. Remove all this waste from the lawn; it will break down gradually if you put it on your compost pile. You can even run the power rake over healthy areas and overseed to create a new mixture of grasses. Check the areas that need to be seeded to make sure that the soil has been disturbed.

If the soil is compacted and doesn't pass the screwdriver test, aerate it.

Now is a good time to add lime and organic fertilizer as indicated by your soil test. A bridge fertilizer, which mixes organics with small amounts of chemicals, is a good choice. Organic matter in the form of compost or peat moss, mixed with topsoil, will help to build up

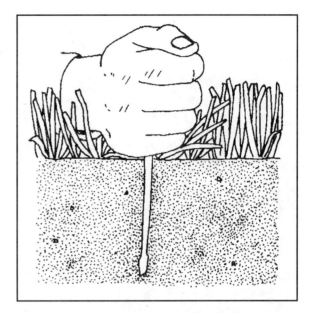

If you're unable to push a screwdriver up to its handle in the ground without hammering on it, your soil is probably compacted and needs aeration.

the soil. Shallow depressions that gather water can be filled with this mixture, although real problem areas might need an improved drainage system. Avoid using high-nitrogen chemical fertilizers during planting, since they can burn the young plants.

The time spent preparing a healthy base for the new seeds will be more than repaid in the future. Before seeding, make sure the area is smooth, level, and has a coarse surface that can later be tamped down to secure the seeds and retain moisture. Then, apply your seed mixture with a lawn seeder or, in small areas, scatter it by hand. Lightly rake the seeds into the surface with a leaf rake, not the rough garden rake you used to prepare the soil. Rake just enough to move the seeds down into the cracks and crevices of the soil surface. Then run a roller over the area to make sure the seeds are in firm contact with the soil.

1. Rough out the surface of the soil with a garden rake (or rent a power rake for larger areas). Remove thatch, weak grass, and weeds.

2. Next, spread on some topsoil mixed with organic matter like peat moss or compost. If your soil needs lime or a little organic fertilizer, work a little into the surface at this time. Smooth out the area to be seeded.

3. Overseed the lawn with a grass seed mixture containing varieties that will thrive in conditions found there (disease-resistant varieties, for instance, or fescues in a shady area that does not favor bluegrass). Gently rake the seeds into the surface of the soil with a broom rake — not a garden rake.

4. Finally, run a roller over the whole area to make sure that the seeds are in firm contact with the soil. Water the area lightly and continue watering as needed over the next few weeks so the seeds do not dry out.

A light watering will get the seeds off to a quick start. It's very important to keep an eye on the moisture for a few weeks. Once seeds are in, they should never be allowed to dry out. When you are overseeding, the cover of existing grass will help to protect the new seeds, but keep an eye on bare patches that you have reseeded.

You can continue with your lawn mowing as normal. For the last mowing of the season, I always cut a little shorter than usual. This prevents the grass from matting down and developing molds over the winter. Meanwhile, your newly seeded grass is getting started and will get a jump on the weed seeds, which usually germinate in the spring.

One last fertilization early in the fall will help get your spruced-up lawn off to a good start in the spring, since it will be storing up energy for that spring growth spurt.

Thatch Isn't Necessary

I have never seen grasses in nature suffer from a thatch problem; all the thatch problems I've ever encountered have been man-made. They are not caused by neglect — far from it. They are simply the result of doing the wrong thing while trying to do the right thing.

The best way to understand thatch is to go out onto the lawn with a knife and cut a two-inch-square plug of lawn and roots. (Don't worry; you can replant it later on.) Look at it in cross-section. If, where the soil ends, there is a layer of tough, fibrous material before the green grass begins, you have thatch. If that layer is only a half-inch thick, I wouldn't worry about it too much. But if it is more than a half-inch thick, it is forming a barrier that will prevent a lot of moisture and fertilization from

reaching the root zone.

That layer of thatch is made up of grass clippings, rhizomes, stolons, and root growth. Your living grass roots may actually be growing in the thatch instead of in the soil, because the soil is hard and unhealthy. Not only does thatch soak up moisture and fertilizer and cause your grass to grow outside the soil, but it is also a dandy breeding ground for some kinds of insects that harm lawns.

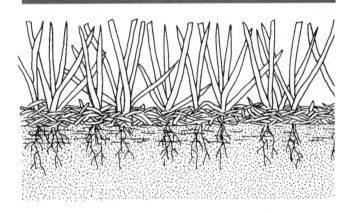

Thatch is a tough, fibrous material that prevents water and nutrients from reaching into the soil and root zone, while offering a haven for destructive insects and other pests.

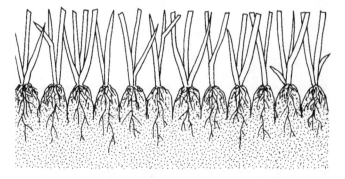

A thatch-free lawn is well-aerated and healthy, with roots reaching deep down into the soil to pick up nutrients and moisture. Near the surface, beneficial soil life breaks down organic matter, feeding the plants and ensuring that thatch will not develop.

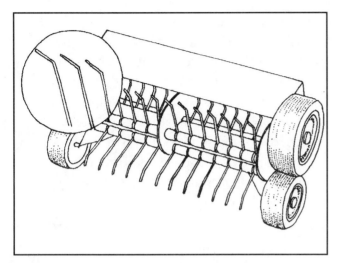

A power rake attachment can be used with a rotary mower to remove thatch from the lawn.

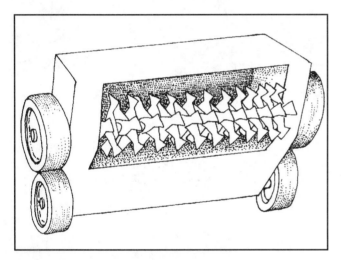

A verticutter operates by lifting the thatch out of the lawn with its vertical blades.

The problem with thatch is not caused by leaving grass clippings on the lawn. On a healthy lawn, grass clippings would be only one-eighth to one-quarter of an inch thick, and they would be loose, not bound together. In healthy soil, grass clippings are broken down and converted to food — up to half of the nitrogen the lawn needs — in just a couple of weeks.

If you wanted to create a terrible thatch problem, here's how you would do it: Use a lot of high-nitrogen chemical fertilizer to promote fast foliage growth, cut the lawn short to discourage deep root growth, and provide regular doses of chemical pesticides to drive out the earthworms and kill off the soil life. In no time at all this lawn would be growing on top of its own growth, which would not have decomposed because the soil would be sickly. That's thatch. And that's what a lot of well-meaning homeowners routinely do to their lawns.

From that list of "don'ts" you should get a pretty good idea of what to do to avoid thatch — just the opposite. But if you have a thick layer of thatch already, a few simple steps should correct the situation. You can either remove the thatch or penetrate the thatch and encourage it to break down.

Thatch can be removed in at least three ways. In small areas, you can simply cut and rake it out with a thatch rake. Power mowers have two means of removing thatch, provided it isn't too thick. One is a special blade for rotary mowers that pulls it out. The other is an attachment for the front of the mower that rakes it out. For severe cases, you can rent or hire a *vertimower* or *verticutter*. This machine operates like a lawn mower, but it has vertical blades that lift the thatch out of the lawn, making it easier for you to rake it up.

Aeration, whether done using a hand tool or a machine, penetrates the thatch by lifting out plugs. In this way air, water, and nutrients can finally get down into the soil. The plugs themselves are left on the lawn to break down and provide some top-dressing. (See the section on aeration starting on page 65).

Top-Dressing

You can encourage the thatch to break down by adding organic matter to the soil — even on top of the thatch. Top-dressing is one way to add organic material. I learned this technique from a golf course greenskeeper. He spread a thin layer of rich, black soil on top of the greens a couple of times a year. The technique takes about three minutes of practice to learn. A big shovel like those used to shovel grain is loaded with dry, organic material or soil, and then swung over the lawn. A sideways flip of the shovel spreads the material, which can be worked in later with a broom rake. Top-dressing with compost is even better, and you needn't worry about a few small lumps since they will either break down by themselves or be broken up by the mower. Compost is full of the soil life that a thatchy lawn so desperately needs. A mixture of compost and peat moss, or one-third vermiculite to two-thirds peat moss, can also be used. Composted manure is especially good, but don't use anything that has been sterilized, since the idea is to add soil life that will help break down the thatch.

Top-dressing is not just a cure for thatch. I have used it in the South on lawns built on topsoil over hard or sandy soils. If left alone, after a while the topsoil just vanishes and the subsoil appears; but top-dressing twice a year can add organic matter from the top down. With the increased interest in organic lawn care, some companies have begun to sell products that can help re-establish soil life.

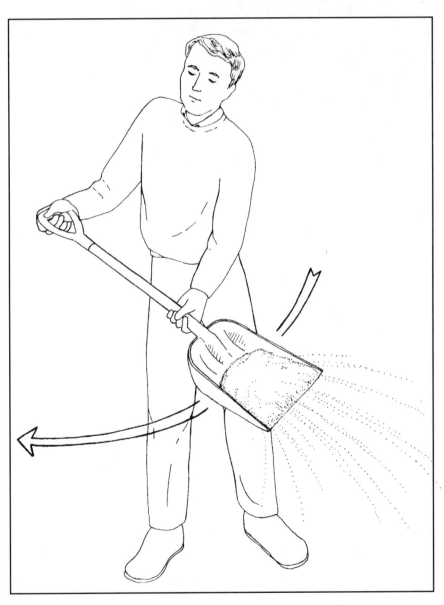

Take a big shovelful of compost and give it sideways flip to distribute it evenly over the lawn. Then rake it in lightly with a broom rake.

Rich, dark compost like this is ideal for top-dressing a lawn.

Once the old thatch has been cleaned up, your lawn-maintenance practices should take over to cure your thatch problem permanently. Wean your lawn from its chemical dependence with an organic or bridge fertilizer. Let the grass grow taller, and never cut more than one-third of the grass at one time. Let the clippings drop and decompose. Gradually your soil will come back to life and your thatch problems will disappear.

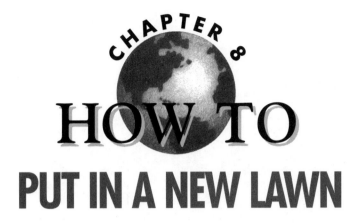

CHAPTER 8

HOW TO

PUT IN A NEW LAWN

I f you are thinking about putting in a new lawn, you are probably in one of two situations: either you have an old lawn that is in such bad shape (more than 50 percent weeds or bare spots) that you are going to tear out what exists and start over, or you are starting with bare ground after a construction project.

Your options are seeding, laying sod, and, with the southern grasses, sprigging or plugging. Personally, I would much rather spend a little extra time putting in a new lawn the right way than spend even more time and money later on to correct problems.

There are a few tricks that can make your life a lot easier for years to come if you think of them before you put in a lawn. For example, I plan the layout of my lawns to avoid those little corner places that are so hard to mow. From a mowing point of view, the best lawn is a big oval. Why not make it that way from the start? You'll probably wind up with a more attractive landscape, too. After all, nothing in nature is perfectly square.

Lawn diseases often start in low spots, where water stands after a rain. Now's the time to make sure the lawn is even and install drainage if necessary. Most important, this is an opportunity to get the soil beneath the lawn into shape. This is also the time to go back to Chapter 2 and plan exactly how you will improve the soil. Take a soil test if you don't have a recent one.

I always begin a gardening project with a big piece of paper so I can make a sketch and note different measurements. For example, your sketch can tell you:

❦ which areas are shady, sunny, play areas, steep hills, or exposed or problem areas, so that you can begin to think about grass seed mixtures or the possibility of using ground covers;

❦ the measurements for buying grass seed, ordering topsoil or sod, planning for your watering system, buying the

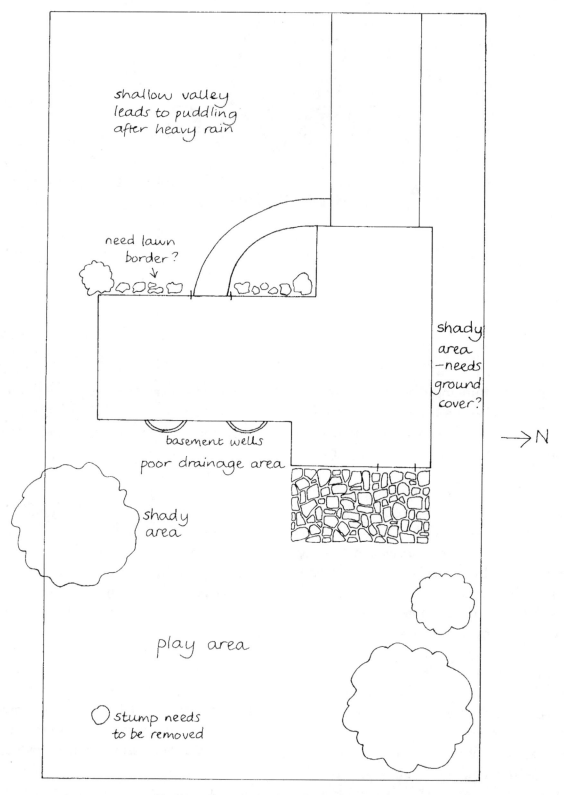

shallow valley
leads to puddling
after heavy rain

need lawn
border?

shady
area
—needs
ground
cover?

→N

basement wells

poor drainage area

shady
area

play area

stump needs
to be removed

Begin your gardening project by making a rough sketch of your landscape, identifying problem spots and taking square foot measurements of any areas for which you'll be ordering grass seed, topsoil, or sod.

I think rototilling is the best way to tear out an old lawn, because it incorporates organic matter into the soil, eliminates weeds, and prepares the site for planting.

right quantities of lime or sulphur, and calculating quantities of soil amendments like fertilizer, peat moss, or manure;

❧ where you might want to install lawn borders to set off the landscaping or keep the lawn from spreading;

❧ where you want to change the grade to improve drainage;

❧ problems, like stumps or cracked walkways, that need attention before

the new lawn gets started.

I always spend some time with a tape measure in addition to analyzing the soil. I also take a tour with a garden cart or wheelbarrow to remove rocks and other objects that will cause problems later on. Sticks, twigs, and old tree root systems are likely to reveal some mushrooms.

Finally, this is the time to decide what kind of grass seed mixture you'll plant. You might want to create different mixes for shady areas — something with more fescue than bluegrass, for example. Make sure now that what you want is available locally. Don't run down to the garden center 10 minutes before you're

Tearing Out an Old Lawn

There are several ways to get rid of an old lawn: poison it; strip it off with a sod cutter; or turn it under with a rototiller, possibly after smothering it with black plastic.

I certainly don't recommend poisoning a lawn, but for many years the common solution was to treat it with a broad-based herbicide containing glyphosate as the active ingredient. The lawn was then shredded with a verticutter and raked up. Landscapers can be hired to handle some or all of this process.

Slicing the old lawn off with a sod cutter is another choice. I first used a sod cutter when doing some work on a golf course. The groundskeeper grew sod in an out-of-the-way area and used it to patch areas on the tees and fairways. A sod cutter has a flat, horizontal blade which is mounted to two vertical struts below. It slices an 18-inch-wide strip out of the lawn, leaving the area below bare for seeding. Unfortunately, it also takes the topsoil in the root zone along with it. If you plan to bring in topsoil anyway, this is just a minor problem.

Rototilling is a third way of getting rid of an old lawn. It's the one I prefer because it leaves the topsoil behind, along with some organic matter that will help restore life to the soil. I plan on going over the area with the rototiller seven times, raking it up, and then waiting a week or so to go over it again and get the clumps that resurface.

There are a couple of ways to prepare the lawn for tilling that make the job a little easier. One is to let the lawn grow out to about six inches, and then cut it as close as you can. This will take a lot of life out of it. Another is to cover the area with black plastic for a few weeks. Or you can apply both methods before tilling. After tilling the second week, carefully rake out all the ruts and bumps. If there has been no rain, a heavy watering a day or two before raking will show you what has been fluffed up by the tiller and what needs to be evened out.

New Lawns

When I establish a new lawn, I treat it just like a vegetable garden. Weeds at the surface should be tilled in, then tilled in again a week later, just before planting the grass seed. I always turn over a garden or lawn just before planting, to knock out weeds that are germinating at the surface.

Step by Step from Bare Ground

Establish a Rough Grade

This is when you fill in low spots, add drainage tile to problem areas, and even out the contours of your lawn. Your house foundation is the primary reference point. Grade the area so that rainwater will drain away from the house, not down the foundation walls. If you have to bring in heavy equipment to get the right grade, push the topsoil off to the side and save it, rather than burying it. Spread it out again when the grading is over.

This is also the time to plan your lawn for easy mowing and to install lawn borders of brick, lumber, plastic, concrete, or whatever your landscape plans call for. If you are going to lay sod, plan ahead for an extra inch of height.

Build the Root Zone

Once the lawn has its overall shape, I look at it from the point of view of the root zone. Are there remaining compacted areas that need aerating before they are planted? How much organic matter can be worked into the soil? You can never have too much. I might bring in some topsoil rich in organic matter; I usually till in half of it to improve the soil, then spread the other half.

Possibly, I'll cover some or all of the area with two inches of wet peat moss and then till it in thoroughly. (To moisten peat moss, cut a hole in the plastic bag and stick a hose into it the night before you want to spread it.) I also might use compost or composted manure, if I have enough. I never use sawdust or bark because it depletes nitrogen from the soil as it decomposes.

Amend the Soil

Now is the time to spread and rake in organic or bridge fertilizers, as well as lime or sulphur, to balance the pH of the soil. Creating the proper pH balance is very important. Without it your lawn can't make full use of the nutrients in the fertilizer you apply, and you will end up wasting a lot of money.

All this preparation and tilling is going to leave your soil fluffed up and in need of a good soaking before you spread the grass seed. This soaking may reveal some dips and humps that will need to be raked out. Then it's time for that one last, very shallow rototilling to knock down weeds.

Seeding

Make sure your seedbed is smooth and level. Go over it with a garden rake if it is not.

The idea is to distribute the seeds evenly and liberally. The two-wheeled spreaders that are used to apply fertilizer also can be used for seeds if they are calibrated to spread the seeds at the recommended rate. By now, you should have calculated how much seed you will need for the area, based on package recommendations and what you know about the square footage of the parcel.

To get an even coverage — about 15 seeds per square inch — I usually set the spreader to apply half the recommended rate, and then spread it in one direction. Then I spread again at right angles to my first pass. This helps to achieve even distribution. Small areas can be seeded by hand from a bucket. Be sure to mix the seed before spreading it, no matter which method you use.

Next, use a garden rake to lightly rake the seeds into the soil. Use a light hand when covering them — they should be buried just an eighth to a quarter of an inch deep. Roll the seeds into firm contact with the ground using a lawn roller. In small areas you can tamp them in with the back of a hoe blade or garden rake.

Keep Seeds Moist

Once the seeds are in place, it is essential to make sure they don't dry out during the germination and early growth stages. A mulch of straw is an old and proven method. (When I say "straw," I'm referring to stalks of grain with the heads harvested.) One good-sized bale should mulch about a thousand square feet. Make sure the straw is clean and does not contain seeds of the grain from which it came. You don't want a field of oats to spring up on your lawn. Hay always contains seeds, so avoid it.

A hand-held broadcast spreader is one way to seed a new lawn.

Man-made fabrics designed specifically for covering newly seeded lawns are now widely available and perform well if you follow instructions. However, they can be tricky to keep in place in windy areas. I go into the closet and get a bunch of coat hangers, then cut and bend them into giant staples that can be pushed through the fabric to hold it down. Just remember to go back and pull them out before you mow the lawn.

Peat moss is fine when mixed into the soil, but it does not make a good mulch. It will actually wick (draw out) moisture from the earth, and it can get crusty. A landscaping fabric that can be left to decompose will do the best job

on steep slopes.

Now that you have put all of this effort into the new lawn, you must make sure to keep the ground moist until the lawn is well established — about two inches long. Probably more lawns and vegetable gardens fail because of germinating seeds that dry out than for any other cause. Of course, once they dry out, they die. As soon as your lawn is in, give it a good, six-inch-deep watering — not just a lick and a promise with the hose. It could take a daily light watering to retain the moisture that your germinating seeds need to grow. This can be just a light sprinkling. In dry, windy conditions, however, it might need a sprinkling more than once a day.

If there are kids around, rope off and mark the newly seeded area. Going out to your new lawn to find footprints or mountain bike tracks can make you very cranky. Even a well-marked new lawn is not dog-proof, however.

Now it's a waiting game. A newly seeded lawn will take two to three weeks to germinate and anywhere from six to ten weeks to get established. Start mowing when the grass is about three inches high.

Installing Sod

Sod lawns are perfect for people who don't mind paying for instant gratification. They look good immediately and can take light use in only a couple of weeks. It's like laying carpet over a plywood floor. Sod will also hold a bank in place, whereas I've seen a newly seeded lawn headed downhill after a sudden rainstorm. But, on the negative side, sod is much more expensive to install than a seeded lawn.

Sod is grown like a crop. You can buy grass mixtures much as you would buy seed mixtures,

Whether you're planting ground cover plants or seeding a new lawn, man-made landscape fabrics offer good protection, as an alternative to straw mulch. Anchor them to the ground by cutting and bending metal coat hangers into giant staples. Just be sure to remove the hangers before your first mowing.

but you may not have as wide a choice as you would with seed. Your local nursery or extension service can help you in your selection. Look for sod that is three-quarters to one inch thick. Despite what you might think, thicker is not better — it's worse, because thick sod has a harder time getting established. Also, avoid sod that has dried out along the edges.

Preparation and speed are the secrets to success with sod. Preparing your site is the same as with seeded lawns, remembering to allow one inch for the extra depth of sod when planning your borders and the edges where it abuts sidewalks and driveways.

Sod should be laid as quickly as possible after it arrives — two or three days in cool weather, and no more than one day in hot weather. If you are delayed, you can stretch it a few days by unrolling the sod onto a hard, flat surface out of the sun and keeping it moist.

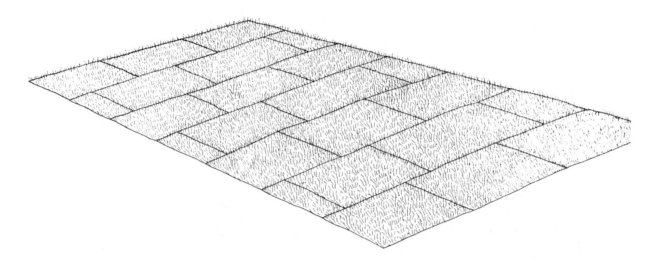

In laying sod, be sure to stagger the starting points of the blocks, to avoid having all of the butt ends form a line. This is especially important when you're laying sod on a slope or bank.

Leaving it rolled up on the pallet can be very costly in terms of damage and dollars. Also, be sure to check the sod when it comes. It should not look faded or yellow.

It pays to plan ahead. The prepared soil should be watered a day or two before the sod is installed to provide a moist, but not muddy, base. Recruit some helpers with strong backs, since pieces of sod may weigh up to 40 pounds.

Start laying sod along a long, straight edge, like a driveway or sidewalk. If you have an irregular shape, stretch a line between two stakes and start at the line. Then work in both directions away from the line. Stagger the starting points so that all the butt ends don't come together in a line. If you are sodding large areas, do one section at a time and then roll and water it before going on to the next.

If you have a hill or a bank, start at the bottom and lay the sod the long way against the bank. On steep banks you can hold it in place with eight-inch pine stakes, leaving them there to decompose, or make giant staples from coat hangers and remove them in a month's time. It is even more important on banks to stagger the strips to make sure the butt ends don't form a straight line, which only invites erosion.

After the sod has been installed, go back and fill in the cracks with topsoil and then roll the whole area. It's important that the sod and the soil below make solid contact. Over time, the sod's root system will knit it into the soil below.

Finally, give your new sod an inch or so of water. Keep an eye on it and water it frequently. You can pick up a corner and look to see if there is moisture at the soil level. As long as you are committed to keeping the sod watered, you can put in a sod lawn at any time of the year (within reason). When it grows to about three inches, give it a mowing.

Sprigs, Plugs, and Sod

If you remember from Chapter 3 how some grasses spread by means of stolons and rhizomes, then planting a lawn with sprigs and plugs will make sense to you. The idea is quite simple and works with nature to create lawns based on the way grasses spread.

Some warm-climate grasses — St. Augustine grass and zoysia grass — are only planted with sprigs, plugs, and sod. These are also the only methods used to plant many varieties of Bermuda grass, although common Bermuda grass can be started from seed.

Sprigs

Bent grass, Bermuda grass, and zoysia grass are commonly planted with sprigs. A *sprig* is a section of stem, long or short, that has at least one joint that will develop into a grass plant. Sprigs come from sod that has been shredded. You can do it yourself or buy sprigs by the bushel. Since warm-climate grasses do best during the heat of the summer, the time to sprig is from late spring to midsummer.

Prepare the soil just as you would for seeding. Keep the sprigs cool and moist until you are ready to plant — the sooner the better — and don't let the stems dry out. Also, the soil should be slightly moist when you get started, so remember to water a day or so ahead.

There are three ways to plant sprigs. The one you choose could depend on the size of the lawn area you are planting.

The quickest way to cover a big area is broadcast sprigging. Sprigs are shredded into short sections and spread like mulch. They are then covered with soil and rolled. Water at least once a day for about a week.

A second method is to spread sprigs out on

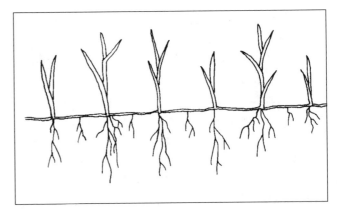

Sprig

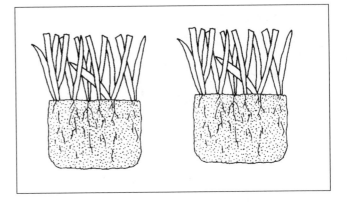

Plugs

a prepared area and then simply push them into the ground with a notched stick. Again, be sure to water them well.

A third method is to make three-inch-deep furrows with a hoe, spaced from four inches to a foot apart in long, parallel lines. The narrower the spacing, the faster the lawn will fill in. Lay the stems in the furrows with the foliage pointed up, then fill in around them with soil. Roll the area and then water frequently.

Plugs

Planting plugs reminds me of planting fall bulbs, and in fact the equipment used is similar. Lawns of St. Augustine, centipede,

Bermuda, and zoysia grass are established using plugs.

Plugs are two- to four-inch chunks of sod, round or square, that are set into holes in a prepared area. You can cut your own plugs from sod, or buy them pre-cut. Plugs of St. Augustine and centipede grass are normally three to four inches in diameter and are set out about a foot apart. Bermuda and zoysia grass are smaller, around two inches in diameter, and are set six to 12 inches apart.

With plugs, as with sprigs, sod, or seed, it is important to prepare the area for planting (see page 102 and following).

Once you're ready to plant, pick up a steel plugger to match the size of the plugs you want to plant. With the plugger, make holes throughout the lawn and press the plugs into them. Keep the plugs cool and moist. They are not as fussy as sprigs, but everything transplants better when both the root system and the hole are moist.

After the plugs have gotten well established, it's a good idea to add soil to the lawn to level it off.

All of these techniques — sodding, sprigging, and plugging — are basically transplanting operations. When I was a youngster, one of the best gardeners around was an old woman named Mazie, who once told me, "You can transplant anything, anytime, as long as you give it plenty of water until it gets going."

If you keep that in mind, you'll have much better luck with your lawn and your garden.

CHAPTER 9

THE BEAUTIFUL LAWN GUIDE
THROUGH THE SEASONS

With a little know-how, the right timing, and a good maintenance program, we can all have beautiful lawns. Let's take a trip through the seasons following in the same order as the calendar year.

In the North, winter is the time when you and your lawn can get a little vacation from each other. The one thing you can do is look ahead to spring with projects like providing drainage for any low spots where water will be likely to stand during the spring thaw. I have some floodplain on my property where I have put in a small golf course, and I've found that early winter, before the deep frost sets in, is a good time to dig a little drainage ditch or install a drainage pipe to move water away from low spots.

In the South, however, the grass will continue to grow in areas where there are few or no freezing days. If you want a green lawn throughout the winter, you can overseed with annual or perennial ryegrass. This is one of the ways that golf courses maintain green lawns during the cool seasons.

Check the schedule below for the best time to add lime or sulphur. If you bring your lawn into the range of about 6.5 pH (see details on page 50), you'll make the maximum use of your fertilizer and improve the life and texture of your soil.

In the Northeast and Midwest (and those transition areas where the fescues and bluegrass are found), it is not a good idea to add chemical fertilizer during the hot days of summer. They can burn the lawn and stimulate weed growth while the lawn goes into its dormancy period. Organic fertilizers, and those bridge fertilizers that contain slow-release chemicals, can be added during the summer in the North and the winter in the South.

Lime can be added at any time, but the best time to add it is after the growth season in the fall. The second best time to add lime is before the growth period begins in the spring.

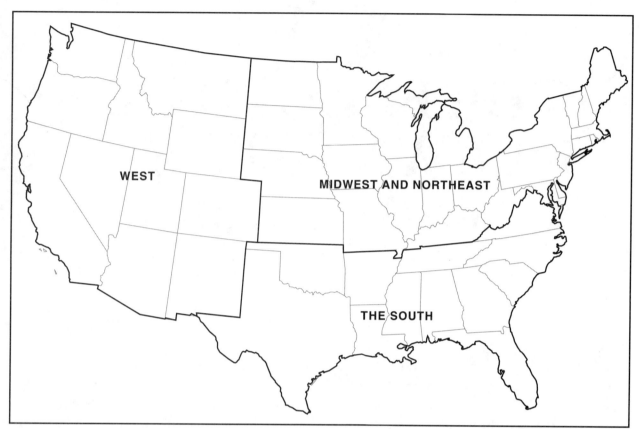

WEST

MIDWEST AND NORTHEAST

THE SOUTH

To simplify seasonal lawn care practices, I've divided the continental United States into three basic maintenance regions. In the pages that follow, you'll find instructions for your own region throughout the course of a typical year.

January—February—March

In the Midwest and Northeast

Take a break, except in the southernmost areas of these regions, where you can get ready to reseed fescues and bluegrass in late March.

1. As the weather allows, use a stiff broom rake to remove dead material and winter debris. Break up lingering snowbanks late in the season to expose the lawn beneath.

2. Apply lime before new growth begins.

In the South

1. Begin fertilizing in the warmest areas.

2. Watch for new growth as the days grow warmer. When it appears, cut the grass above it to open it up to the warmth and light.

3. Repair damaged areas by resodding, sprigging, or plugging.

4. If you have chosen to use chemicals on problem weeds, you should apply them as the temperatures nudge up into the mid-60s and new growth is about to begin.

5. Add lime if necessary.

In the West

1. In southern areas of the region, begin fertilizing. This is the time to plant new lawns.

2. In areas where cool-season grasses are present, you can begin fertilizing as the days warm up in March.

3. Remove thatch before the new growing season begins.

4. If you've gone the chemical route, as days warm up use the pre-emergent herbicides to control crabgrass and broad-leaved weeds.

5. If you live in a southern part of the region and have overseeded for the winter with annual ryegrass, cut the winter grass short as the days warm up to expose the lawn below to heat and light.

6. Add lime, if necessary.

7. Shampoo the lawn. (See step number 7, on the following page.)

April—May

In the Midwest and Northeast

1. As the temperatures creep up toward the 70s, you are entering the best time of the year for seeding and sodding new lawns, and for spring fertilization. The lawn is about to enter its heartiest growth spurt of the year, beginning when the temperatures hit the mid-70s.

2. After the frost goes out of the ground, you can flatten frost bumps with a roller half-filled with water and also roll fall-seeded lawns.

3. When the frost is completely out of the ground, reseed or sod damaged areas.

4. Remove thatch before growth starts.

5. If you are into chemical herbicides, add pre-emergent chemicals before new growth appears, and apply post-emergent chemicals for broad-leaved weeds as they begin to show growth.

6. If you live in the transition areas that have some broad-leaved grasses like Bermuda grass, and have overseeded with annual rye for the winter, mow the winter grass to open up the established lawn for new growth.

7. Shampoo the lawn. My bug- and disease-prevention program at this time of the year calls for spraying liquid soap (not detergent) and water on the lawn. This is one of the few times I use a hose-end sprayer, since accuracy is not as critical when applying soap as it is with other chemicals. The mixture is two ounces of soap per gallon of water. It helps prevent and clear up diseases like snow mold. I don't know exactly why, but I do know that the fatty acids in the soap will attack some insects. I apply it when the grass is dry and there is no forecast of rain for a few days. I spray twice, about a month apart, and give the lawn two more shampoos in the fall.

In the South

1. Warming weather makes this the time to plant grasses that have their big growth period during the hot days of summer: Bermuda grass, St. Augustine grass, and the other warm-climate grasses can be started from seed, sprigs, or plugs (as is appropriate for the type).

2. Remove thatch early.

3. Fertilize.

4. As broad-leaved weeds such as dandelions begin growing, dig or pull them up or apply post-emergent chemical controls.

In the West

1. If you live in a cool-season grass area, you can fertilize if you have not already done so, or if heavy rains have washed the fertilizer away.

2. Now's the time to plant Bermuda grass and other warm-season grasses by seed, sprig, or plug. These will hit their big growth spurt when the temperatures top 80°F (27°C), while the northern grasses start growing when the temperature reaches the 70s and tend to go dormant during the hot weather. You want to have them planted and germinating for their big growth periods.

3. Early in the period, remove thatch.

4. If you have overseeded an annual winter grass, do not fertilize early while it is still growing, or it may grow at the expense of the lawn beneath it. Mow annual grasses short to open up the lawn below.

5. Dig or pull up broad-leaved weeds like dandelions, or apply post-emergent chemicals to control them as they begin to show growth.

June

In the Midwest and Northeast

1. Your fertilizing should be done except in southern coastal or transitional areas where grasses from the South are present. Northern grasses may start to go dormant.

2. If you are using chemicals, you might still want to spot-spray individual problem areas.

3. Armyworms and chinch bugs may be attacking your lawn. If so, try to identify the culprit or take it to a garden center and have an expert look it over.

4. Mow, mow, mow — but never more than one-third the height of the grass at a time.

In the South

1. Fertilize.

2. Water.

3. Mow, but set the mower an inch higher this month.

4. Battle chinch bugs, webworms, and armyworms.

5. If you are using chemicals, crabgrass may be hit with a post-emergent herbicide at this time.

In the West

1. Fertilize southern grasses, but hold off on fertilizing bluegrasses and fescues, since they will soon be going into their dormant period.

2. Mow, but set the mower an inch higher this month.

3. If using chemicals, spot-spray for crabgrass.

4. Keep an eye out for insect damage. Identify and control.

July—August

In the Midwest and Northeast

1. If you want a green lawn all summer long, remember to water. I don't water until the lawn clearly needs it, because I want to encourage the roots to go deep in search of water. When I do

water, however, I make sure I give it at least an inch and that the water penetrates the soil deeply — about six inches into the root zone. Shallow watering is worse than no watering at all.

2. By mid-August you will be going into another good time to start a new lawn with cool-season grasses.

3. In transition areas with southern grasses, continue fertilizing.

In the South

1. Southern grasses, like Bermuda and zoysia grass, enjoy being fertilized in either of these months.

2. Mow, but keep the mower set high.

3. Water.

In the West

1. Fertilize southern grasses but not northern grasses.

2. Northern grasses must be watered if you want to keep them green. Southern grasses need deep watering to sustain them through this peak growth period.

3. Mow, keeping the mower set high.

September

In the Midwest and Northeast

1. The return of cool weather sends northern grasses into their second seasonal growth period.

2. Fertilize now, so your lawn can store energy for the spring growth period. This is the most important time to fertilize.

3. Late August and early September, depending upon your climate, are good times to start a new lawn or repair damaged areas. Time it so that the lawn will just be getting established as the fall growth period begins.

4. Fall is the very best time to apply lime to lawn and gardens. Rain and snow will wash it into the soil, and it can begin to go to work in the spring.

5. Young, broad-leaved weeds that have found their way into your lawn are now gaining a

foothold. If you are using chemicals, now is a good time to control them, before they have a chance to reappear next spring.

6. In southern transitional areas, overseed Bermuda grass with annual ryegrass for a green winter lawn.

7. If you have had a thatch problem this year, dethatch before the fall growth period begins, so the lawn will have a chance to recover.

In the South

1. Another month for fertilizing. This may be the last month of the summer in areas except for the far South. In northern transition areas, where bluegrass and fescues make up part of the lawn, this is the beginning of the time for the fall fertilization, which is the most important for the northern grasses.

2. In transition areas, this is also a great time to start a lawn of cool-season grasses.

3. In cooler areas of the South, this is the time for that all-important application of lime.

4. If you have a problem with annual bluegrass, now is the time to apply a pre-emergent chemical control.

In the West

1. Except for the southernmost areas, this is a fine time to start a lawn of the cool-climate grasses.

2. Fertilize established grasses, particularly the northern fescues and bluegrasses.

3. Remove thatch, and fertilize after the job is done, not before.

4. Apply a pre-emergent chemical herbicide if you have a problem with annual bluegrass.

October—November—December

In the Midwest and Northeast

1. In southern areas there is still a little time left early in the period to establish new lawns, fertilize, and use chemical weed controls.

2. Cleanup and rake-up time.

3. Apply lime.

4. In northern grass areas, you may still have time early in the period for the important fall fertilization.

5. I usually give the lawn another shampoo early in October just like in the spring (see step 7 on page 112).

In the South

1. There's time for one last fertilization in southern areas where Bahia, Bermuda, St. Augustine, and zoysia grasses make up your lawn.

2. For a green lawn during the winter, overseed the soon-to-be-dormant Bermuda grass with annual ryegrass.

3. A young crop of broad-leaved weeds may emerge this time. Control with post-emergent chemicals, if you choose.

In the West

1. For those with cool-season grasses in southern or transition areas, you could start a new lawn as late as November.

2. The last fertilization of the season for southern grasses occurs early in this period.

3. Add lime or sulphur as required.

4. Cleanup and rake-up time.

CHAPTER 10

WHAT'S THAT
BROWN PATCH?

I HATE TO SOUND LIKE A NAG, but if you had put your efforts into building healthy soil, and developed a maintenance program that includes proper watering, mowing, and fertilization, you probably wouldn't have to read this chapter at all. Lawn diseases usually are found on lawns that have been pushed toward perfection with regular doses of chemical fertilizers, herbicides, and even fungicides, which are supposed to be the cure, but are often part of the problem.

My solution is simple and cheap. Twice a year, spring and fall, I give the lawn a shampoo. It prevents a lot of bug and disease problems. The fatty acids in soap will kill some bugs, the same as insecticidal soaps, and the treatment seems to work on snow mold and other diseases as well. I use about two ounces of liquid Ivory soap to a gallon of water. Other liquid soaps will also work, but don't use detergents. I give the lawn two shampoos, about a week apart, as growth begins in spring, and again in the fall after the growth period is over.

Certainly everyone will have the occasional brown spot caused by pet urine, an oil or gasoline spill, or a spill of chemical fertilizer. Cleaning up and flushing the area with water is all that's required. In the case of gas or oil, flushing with soapy water will help break up the mess.

I look at lawn diseases about the same way as I look at "bugs" likes colds and flu that affect humans. The bugs are always around, but the person who eats right, exercises, and gets enough sleep is likely to avoid them. Stressed-out people who burn the candle at both ends seem more vulnerable to them.

The connection between lawn diseases and chemical usage are even clearer. The kind of high-nitrogen fertilization that creates excessive foliage growth at the expense of root growth can cause thatch buildup, and result in weakened plants. Organic and bridge fertilizers avoid this kind of problem. Thatch is a problem because it becomes a nesting ground for diseases and bugs, and it can prevent ad-

Brown patch is the most common lawn disease, often appearing as irregular circles on lawns that have been overloaded with high-nitrogen chemical fertilizers.

Some fungi are always present in your lawn, and may appear under favorable climatic conditions. Mushrooms like these can actually be good news — indicating a healthy amount of organic matter in the soil. Even if you see the symptoms of a fungal disease, though, don't reach for a chemical quick-fix. Often the problem can be controlled through normal maintenance practices.

equate water and fertilization from reaching the roots.

Chemicals can also damage the microbial plant life that helps battle disease. I think of the soil life as similar to our white blood cells that fight infection. This soil life is part of the soil's immune system. In fact, microorganisms in the soil compete with fungi for food, so, when they are abundant, the diseases are kept in check. But when they are weakened, diseases have an open invitation to invade.

A variety of fungi that cause plant diseases are always present in your lawn, but for them to get a strong foothold they need some favorable conditions. These include temperature; the right amount of (or absence of) sunlight; moisture, or the lack of it; and a type of grass that doesn't resist the fungus.

My point is, when you see that mysterious spreading brown splotch, don't automatically rush to the garden store to buy a fungicide. Sometimes it takes a close inspection to determine whether it is an insect or a disease that is causing the problem. Simply spraying household soap on the area might do the job.

Another good reason to go slow on fungicide application is that, by the time the damage is visible, the conditions necessary for fungus growth may have changed and the problem may clear up by itself.

Be a Lawn-Disease Detective

Lawn diseases are tricky to identify. Some scientists spend their entire careers researching and identifying fungi that cause diseases, but you don't have to be an expert to do a little basic detective work. Here's how I do it.

1. Take an overall look at the damage. Does it appear round? Irregular? Large? Small? What color is the damage? Do the colors change from the center to the edges? Is this insect damage or a disease?

Dollar spot is often found on lawns where excess moisture and thatch buildup are a problem.

2. Take a close look at the problem. An entire world exists just below our ability to see it with the naked eye. A handy thing to have around the house and garden is a photographer's loupe. This is a little magnifying glass that artists and photographers use to examine the details of negatives. They are designed so that they stand by themselves at just the right distance to focus on the object on which they are standing. They are perfect for examining tiny bugs, egg clusters, and grass and plant damage. You can buy one in a photo or art supply store. Some clues on what to look for are listed below among the disease descriptions.

3. Make a note of the outdoor conditions. At what time of the year did the problem first appear? Does it come back every year at the same time? Is it hot? Cold? Does it show up as the snow melts? Does water stand in this spot?

Does it appear in the sun or in the shade? Does it show up where trees or shrubs are close to the ground and prevent air circulation? What kind of grass is it attacking?

4. What are the soil conditions? Dry? Hard and compacted from traffic? Do you know if the soil has a pH in the 6.0 to 7.0 range, which is best for grass?

Armed with this information, you have a pretty good chance of figuring out what the problem is and taking the appropriate action — if, indeed, any action is required at all.

Descriptions of Some Common Lawn Diseases

Brown Patch

Brown patch should be your first suspect, since it is the most common lawn disease. It is found all over the country except in the Pacific Northwest and affects both warm- and cool-climate grasses.

Clues: It appears in July and August when temperatures climb to the 75° to 95°F (24° to 35°C) range and the humidity is high. It is likely to show up on lawns fertilized with high-nitrogen chemicals, ones that have also developed thatch. It appears as large, irregular circles several feet across. They turn brown or gray, and the edges of the patch may look waterlogged. Upon close examination, you may see the grass turning brown from the top down, and brown patches may appear on the faded grass. Poor drainage often contributes to brown patch.

Controls: Avoid high-nitrogen fertilizers. Clear trees or brush to reduce shade, and remove thatch. Water deeply to get moisture through the thatch and down into the root zone. Improve drainage by top-dressing to add organic matter, or, in chronic cases, rebuild the area to improve drainage.

Dollar Spot

Dollar spot gets its name because it first appears in spots about the size of a silver dollar, but it could be much larger by the time you notice it because the spots merge and grow.

Clues: There is a tan-colored, dollar-sized spot. It likes moderate temperatures and can appear from May to November. It is likely to develop where there is excess moisture and heavy thatch. It will infect all grasses, but is particularly a problem for bent grass and Bermuda grass. Under close examination you may see white, fluffy strands on the leaves when it is moist, as in the morning.

Controls: Unlike most diseases, dollar spot often shows up where grass has not been fertil-

ized, so a gentle feeding of nitrogen can help. Remove thatch and water deeply. Regular high mowing can cut off the infected tips.

Fusarium Patch

Fusarium patch, also called **pink snow mold**, is a cool-weather problem that shows up from fall through spring. In the North it is often found under or around melting snowbanks.

Clues: White or pink circular patches one to eight inches across when conditions are between 40° and 60°F (4° to 16°C) and moist. It can infect most cool-climate grasses and zoysia grass. You may see threads of fungus under close examination, especially in the morning.

Controls: Avoid high-nitrogen fertilizers. Reduce shade if you can, aerate and remove thatch. Improve drainage by top-dressing with organic matter or rebuilding.

Leaf Spot

Leaf spot is sometimes called **melting-out**. It is really a number of similar diseases that appear when temperatures are cool 50° to 70°F (10° to 21°C) and conditions are moist. It is usually found in certain varieties of Kentucky bluegrass, as well as in Bermuda grass and fescues, although the various strains can be found on all types of grasses. Gray leaf spot infects new St. Augustine grass lawns.

Clues: Long, roughly circular spots appear in the shade and spread. Spots are light brown to brown in the center, with black to purple edges. Close examination will reveal brown to black splotches on the leaves.

Controls: Avoid high-nitrogen fertilizers. Keeping the grass cut too short seems to encourage leaf spot, so keep the mower set high and remove clippings. Try to reduce the shaded area if possible. Aerate and improve drainage.

Powdery Mildew

Powdery mildew shows up as patches of dusty white or gray powder on the grass, often in shady areas where the air circulation is poor. It is usually not a big threat to your lawn. It appears from midsummer to November.

Controls: If possible, reduce the shade and improve air circulation by pruning trees and shrubs. Don't water or fertilize.

Pythium Blight

Pythium blight is sometimes called *grease spot* or *cottony blight,* and can be a problem on newly established lawns. Once it strikes, it moves fast and can do a lot of damage. Bent grass, Bermuda grass, bluegrass, tall fescue, and ryegrass are all vulnerable, and there are no resistant grasses.

Clues: In the morning, look for a white or gray fungus covering brown, diseased areas. They may look water-soaked. This is a disease of hot, humid conditions. Diseased areas may range in size from a few inches to a few feet. It often appears on closely cut lawns.

Controls: It is best prevented by maintaining a proper pH balance in the soil. It will go away in dry weather. Avoid overwatering in hot weather and go light on fertilizers. If possible, open up infected areas to sunlight and air circulation.

Red Thread

Red thread likes the moist, cool weather of spring and fall. It is found most often in the Northeast and Pacific Northwest. It shows up as small, dead patches.

Clues: Close examination in the morning or under wet conditions will reveal bright pink threads of fungus. It is sometimes called *pink patch.*

Controls: Increase nitrogen fertilization, and include frequent high mowing.

Rust

Rust, as its name suggests, makes the infected lawn look rusty from a distance. It does not cause major damage. Like most turf diseases, it likes moist conditions and moderately warm weather.

Controls: Speed up growth by applying nitrogen fertilizer and then mow every five days.

SAD

SAD, or St. Augustine Grass Decline, is not a fungus, but a virus, that attacks St. Augustine grass in Texas and Louisiana. It causes lawns to yellow and weakens them until they are invaded by weeds or Bermuda grass.

Controls: Not much can be done except to plant resistant varieties such as Floralawn, Floratam, Raleigh, Seville, and Tamlawn.

Stripe Smut

Stripe smut likes the cool, moist weather of spring and fall and attacks Kentucky bluegrass and bent grass. As the disease advances, grass deteriorates.

Clues: Close inspection will show long, black stripes of spores on grass leaves that are paler in color than they should be. Shriveled, shredded leaves indicate the final stage.

Controls: Avoid overwatering and conditions that encourage thatch.

Summer Patch

Summer patch, and a related disease called *necrotic ring spot,* are typical turf diseases that show up as brown areas that spread. Grass that is stressed by high traffic or weather conditions may show the problem first. Unlike most turf diseases, it likes hot, dry, breezy conditions (although necrotic ring spot is a cool-climate disease). It infects bluegrass, tall fescue, and annual ryegrass.

Clues: A dead giveaway is the appearance of a "frog's-eye" pattern in the grass. This is a large area in which a brown circle, sometimes not completely closed into a circle, surrounds a green and healthy patch of grass. At this stage, they are several feet across.

Controls: Start with the basic practices for good lawn care: use organic or bridge fertilizers; keep your mower set high; and plant a good grass mixture in the beginning. Light watering during drought instead of deep watering is the one break you should make with normal maintenance routines.

Although there are hundreds of possible diseases, there is one message I think you can now see: quick fixes are no real substitute for simple, basic practices that put you in harmony with nature.

If soap sprays and other practices don't solve the problem, you may have to resort to using a fungicide. Fungicides either work from within the plant (systemic) or on the outside of the plant as a preventive step. The latter is what soap spraying does. If I have to use a fungicide, I try to use a systemic one, since it works only on a narrow range of plants. This is where your detective work comes into play. If you can identify the problem, you can choose a fungicide that best suits the purpose. Your garden supply center can be of help here.

A cure may take time, so be patient. In hot, humid climates, though, be less patient, because those conditions encourage the rapid spread of fungi. If the lawn is severely damaged, you can make repairs (see Chapter 7). Make sure you reseed with disease-resistant varieties.

How to Prevent Problems

I'll bet you've heard one of my favorite expressions: "Never time to do it right; always time to do it over." Every gardener, home repairer, painter, and carpenter that has any experience at all will nod in agreement with that idea. When painting, spend most of the time preparing the surface. When building, measure twice, cut once. When growing things, take time to build the soil. Here's how I prevent turf disease problems:

1. Choose resistant varieties (see the section beginning on page 35, which lists some disease-resistant grass varieties).

2. Plant a mixture of grasses to increase the chances of one or more types surviving and prospering. This helps to balance out requirements for sun and shade, too. Choose grasses that are right for the job; choices for a front yard can be different from choices for play areas.

3. Take the time to build a good soil base when installing a new lawn (see Chapter 8).

4. Understand and correct your soil's pH balance. This is easy to do by spreading lime or sulphur. Poor pH balance can prevent soils from using the fertilizer you apply.

5. Don't overfertilize.

6. Mow properly, which means don't cut more than one-third of the growth. A short lawn often is stressed and vulnerable to disease. A sharp lawn mower blade will not leave ragged leaves that invite disease.

7. Don't remove clippings. Let them break down to feed the lawn nitrogen and organic matter. The exception is in the case of diseased lawns, where you should remove diseased material and dispose of it where it won't infect a new area.

8. Top-dress with organic materials to improve lawns that have been on chemical treatment for extended periods. This can also help improve drainage.

9. Low spots where puddles form are invitations to disease. Watch out for low spots when installing a new lawn. In an established lawn, it may be necessary to rebuild in order to improve drainage. Top-dressing might help.

10. In problem areas like steep banks, consider ground covers instead of grass.

11. Don't overwater, but, when you do water, make sure you do so deeply enough to penetrate the soil into the root zone.

12. Remove thatch. It is associated with several lawn diseases and prevents water and fertilizers from penetrating into the root zone.

13. Avoid fungicides. They are hard on soil life. If you must spray, try a biodegradable household dish soap.

14. Stay out of diseased areas when they are wet. You can easily drag the fungus around and spread it.

In the very first chapter, I mentioned that it is just as important to know what not to do. Trying to create a picture-perfect lawn by relying on chemicals is definitely one of the things *not* to do. It only creates the conditions that encourage disease.

CHAPTER 11

BUGS

IN THE GRASS

Even if you don't like bugs, you'll have to admit they have at least one redeeming feature — they provide food for birds. So, in our rush to kill bugs, we've applied pesticides that harm our birds and, in some cases, the fish population.

I don't worry very much about insects on my lawn. They aren't a big problem, so there's no need to run for the pesticide can every time you see one. Unless there is an enormous infestation of some very specific kind of insect, you can leave them alone. My approach is to use only as much force as necessary, as you'll see below, and to try to find out exactly what I'm dealing with, so I can use specific controls and not kill everything in sight.

If I do finally resort to pesticides, I try to stick with organic ones. The lawn is an incredibly efficient filter, so using pesticides and fungicides in moderation is not going to cause any major problems. Always read the label and follow the manufacturer's instructions very carefully before using any pesticide. This is one thing everyone can do for the environment. Homeowners typically use much too much pesticide on their lawns, yet they often point a finger at farmers for spraying chemicals. By comparison, homeowners use far more.

It's not true that every good bug is a dead bug. Without bees, for instance, our crops would not be pollinated and many plants would not produce. And, as every serious gardener knows, many insects feed on the bugs that damage our lawns and gardens.

After years of watching nature's cycles on my lawn and garden, I can almost always identify insects by the kind of damage they cause.

The Bugs in Your Lawn

Dozens, even hundreds, of different kinds of insects live in your lawn and yet just a few need our attention. Only a handful of bugs that can be found in the lawn are really capable of destroying it. They are the grubs, chinch bugs, and webworms.

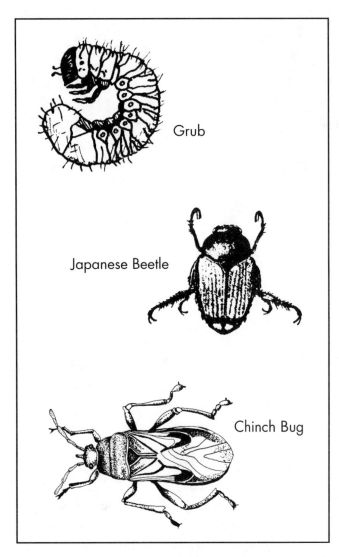

Grub

Japanese Beetle

Chinch Bug

a golf ball. These are caused by skunks or raccoons digging for grubs under the surface. Mole tunnels may also appear, since an infestation of grubs will attract moles to your lawn.

If, during the summer, you see many metallic-looking, green-and-bronze-colored beetles (Japanese beetles) eating your flowers or vegetables, you will have some grubs. Japanese and many other kinds of beetles lay their eggs in the soil. The eggs become grubs, which in turn become beetles and pop up out of the lawn.

If an area appears to be badly damaged by grubs, I slide a spade under the turf and roll it back, almost like rolling up a rug. It should come up easily. If there are more than a few grubs per square foot, it is time to take action.

Natural Controls. Expose the grubs to the air by turning back the sod and let the birds clean them up.

There are also several organic controls available. A thorough application of milky spore disease (*Bacillus popilliae*) should keep grubs at bay for several years, since infected grubs produce more of the spore. To be effective, follow the directions very carefully. Grub controls are commercially available under the trade names Scanmask and Biosafe. These spray on and actually contain millions of microscopic parasitic nematodes.

I don't use Japanese beetle traps because I think they attract beetles into the garden from the entire neighborhood. Try hand-picking any beetles you find and dropping them into a jar of water with a little kerosene or soap in it.

Chemical Controls. Look for pesticides containing chlorpyrifos, diazinon, isofenphos, or trichlorfon.

If your lawn is showing signs of damage, make a close inspection of the area and bring back one of the culprits in a jar for identification; that is, if you can actually find the guilty bug.

Grubs

Their damage shows up in the late spring or early fall as irregular brown patches. Grubs can be very damaging because they actually chew the roots off the grass and then keep going. One sign of grubs in your lawn is the appearance, overnight, of holes about the size of

Chinch Bugs

These bugs cause large, round patches in the lawn, which are yellow in the center and greenish toward the edges as they expand. They are found in sunny areas of the lawn. St. Augustine grass is particularly vulnerable, although Kentucky bluegrass and bent grass may also get hit. Chinch bugs operate above the ground and suck the juice out of the grass stems. They are tiny.

I test for chinch bugs by cutting both ends out of a tin can and pushing it into an affected area — not the dead yellow part, but the part where damage is still underway and the grass shows some green. Fill the can with water. Chinch bugs, if they are around, will float to the top.

Natural controls. Some types of St. Augustine grass are resistant, so plant these. Keep the lawn free of thatch, which these pests seem to love. Diatomaceous earth (which consists of the tiny sharp skeletons of one-celled algae) is effective against a wide range of insects, including chinch bugs. Don't buy the kind that is sold for use in swimming pools, though.

I have found that spraying soapy water on infected areas every two weeks or less can be very effective. The botanical insecticide sabadilla can also be used to control chinch bugs. Be careful when you apply it, though, because sabadilla dust can irritate the nose, throat, and eyes.

Webworms

Sod webworms come out at night and chew the grass off just above the thatch. They pull the grass into their web nest to eat it. The damage shows up in late spring or summer as one- or two-inch dead patches among the grass.

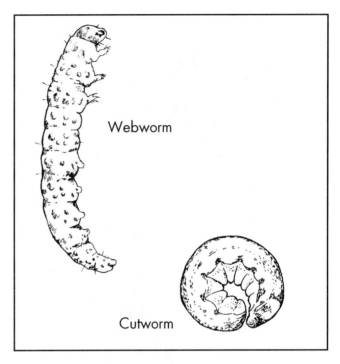

Webworm

Cutworm

Break up these dead spots to see if you can find light brown caterpillars and their nests. Birds and moles feeding on the lawn are a sign of webworms. The caterpillars come from the eggs of a light brown moth that flies a few inches above the lawn at dusk and drops eggs like bombs.

Natural controls. Soapy water; insecticidal soaps; or *Bacillus thuringinsis* (Bt).

Cutworms

These can be a big problem for vegetable gardeners because they come out at night, wrap their bodies around transplants, and cut them off just above the ground. They do the same thing to grass. You often find them in the soil, curled up tightly like a sleeping cat.

Natural controls. Parasitic nematodes or diatomaceous earth. Bt will also knock out some types of cutworms.

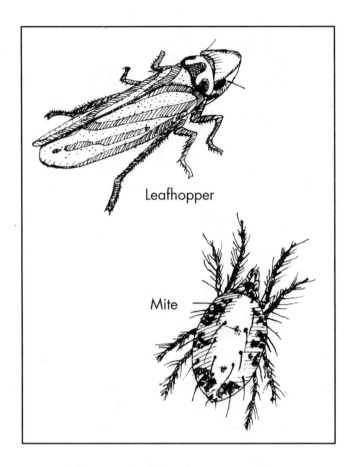

Leafhopper

Mite

Natural controls. Parasitic nematodes attack billbugs in the larval stage. The botanical insecticide rotenone can be either sprayed or dusted on billbugs as a control.

Chemical controls. Try midsummer applications of a product containing diazinon.

Greenbugs

Greenbugs are tiny members of the aphid family that suck sap from the blades of grass and deposit a poison. The damage appears as rust-colored spots in shady areas that spread as the infestation increases. Although greenbugs are small, a major infestation can threaten an entire lawn. You can spot greenbugs by a close-up examination of the damaged areas. They like Kentucky bluegrass.

Natural controls. Ladybugs and lacewing larvae are natural insect predators of all aphids and will eat greenbugs. I've also had good luck with insecticidal soap on all kinds of aphid problems.

Leafhoppers

These tiny green, yellow, or gray flying bugs will cause a lawn to look bleached out if there is a major infestation. Their greatest threat is to new lawns. It is rare for an infestation to get to the point that chemical use is necessary. There are always some around, but if you have a major problem you'll kick up a little cloud of them as you scuff through the grass.

Natural controls. Pyrethrum, a botanical insecticide, is available at most garden centers in a spray or dust form.

Chemical controls. Pesticides containing carbaryl or diazinon are effective. Children should be kept off areas treated with diazinon for several days after application.

Billbugs

These bugs are named for their long snouts. You might spot some on paved areas early in the summer. However, it is not the bugs that do the damage. It is their larvae, which feed underground on roots. They are fairly small, about the size of puffed rice kernals. Grass turns yellow or brown in a circle, and the dead area is easy to lift out, just as it is in any grub-damaged area. The damage shows up in late summer.

Mites

There are a variety of these tiny pests, which are eight-legged arachnids, related to ticks and spiders. You will notice their damage (curled, dry, or yellowed grass) before you see the mites. Different varieties attack clover, bluegrass, fescues, and Bermuda grass. They are sucking insects and may live on the underside of leaves.

Natural controls. Spray with an insecticidal soap.

Mole Crickets

These are burrowing crickets, found in the South, whose damage shows up as streaks of brown and wilted grass. They are large — up to two inches long — and they feed on grass roots. Their tunneling causes roots to be exposed and dry out, and damaged areas will lift out of the lawn easily. You may be able to feel or see their tunnels.

Natural controls. Parasitic nematodes or milky spore disease (*Bacillus popilliae*).

Chemical controls. Mole cricket bait containing propoxur or a pesticide containing diazinon.

Slugs and Snails

These aren't insects, but mollusks (the landlubber cousins of clams and mussels). They come out at night to eat and hide in cool, shady places during the day. They will do some damage to dichondra and other ground covers, but really prefer vegetable gardens.

Natural controls. Pick them by hand. Shake

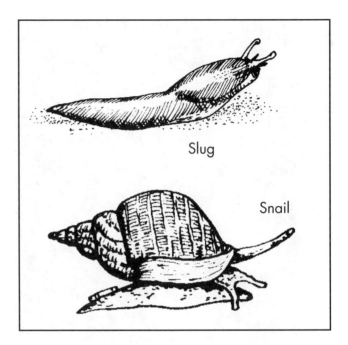

Slug

Snail

salt on them and watch them fizz. Diatomaceous earth, lime, or wood ashes will keep them back. Some people trap them in saucers of beer set into the garden, but you would need a lot of beer to keep them out of large areas.

How I Deal with Insect Pests

There's no need to run for the pesticide can every time you see a bug. My approach is to start with good gardening techniques and then use only as much force as necessary to deal with any problems that show up. Let me give you some examples of what I mean.

First, if you pay attention to building healthy soil, a lot of insect and plant disease problems will never bother you. Insects and diseases usually attack plants that are weak, damaged, or stressed. Some insects, for example, thrive where there is thatch. Thatch results from overfertilization with strong chemicals, which also knocks out a lot of important soil life. Build healthy soil.

Putting up bathouses may not be for everyone, but many folks swear by these real-life caped crusaders, who gobble up hordes of insects. Courtesy Gardeners Supply Co.

Bugs comes in all sizes, shapes, and colors, but basically they all do their damage in one of three ways:

❧ They eat leaves or suck plant juices from the stems. These pests, like greenbugs, webworms, mites, leafhoppers, armyworms and chinch bugs, are frequent problems on lawns.

❧ They feed from within the stems (more of a problem in vegetable gardens than with lawns).

❧ They attack below or at ground level. Grubs and cutworms fall into this category. If you get rid of grubs, you will very likely solve your mole, skunk, and raccoon problems, too.

If you can't find the bug causing the damage, try a sneak attack. Go out after dark with a flashlight and check the damaged areas. Bring back a specimen for identification.

Fourth, good housekeeping around the yard and garden can eliminate problems before they begin. I get rid of infected plants quickly and far away from my yard. Burn them if you are allowed. Don't give bugs a chance to winter over and breed by allowing vegetable gardens to stand all winter. Turn organic matter back into the soil. Keep lawns mowed to the proper length. Keep them properly watered. A well-managed compost pile won't attract insects, but organic matter left lying around to decompose will attract them.

Fifth, encourage birds to visit your yard. Install a martin house or put a birdbath in the yard. If you're not squeamish about these unloved and misunderstood creatures, encourage bats and toads to hang around by building bat houses and toad hideouts (an old broken flower

Second, you can prevent a lot of lawn and garden insect problems by knocking pesky bugs, like Japanese beetles, into a jar of water with a little kerosene or soap in it. If you don't like picking them up, I suggest using an old fork from the kitchen to knock them into the jar, scooping them up, or, if all else fails, stabbing them to death.

Third, if you get to know your bugs, you will be able to choose a remedy that solves your problem without harming beneficial insects.

pot turned upside down will attract toads). These beneficial critters devour insects by the thousands.

Natural Controls and Pesticides

More and more "organic" insect controls are beginning to appear on the market. Although many of them are made for vegetable gardeners, they can be just as useful around the lawn and landscape. One advantage of some organic pesticides is that they are specific to one kind of bug problem and do not harm other, beneficial insects. Organic pesticides break down faster than most chemical pesticides, but they still can be potent, and require careful use. Some natural controls use natural enemies, or take advantage of a pest's vulnerability to specific diseases. Since they work differently, I have grouped them.

Household and Insecticidal Soaps

Many household soaps have mild insecticidal characteristics because they contain fatty acids. Insecticidal soaps, the best-known of which are marketed by Safer, are compounded to make maximum use of fatty acids as an insecticide. Fatty acids break down within 48 hours into potassium, carbon dioxide, and water, all harmless. They kill bugs by penetrating their shells and draining away fluids.

Safer has more than 50 products on the market, some of them combining fatty acids with other organics like pyrethrins and Bt, which have different characteristics. The basic soap will not kill ladybugs or honeybees. It is used to control aphids, greenbugs, lace bugs, squash bug nymphs, leafhoppers, thrips, scale,

A broken flowerpot turned upside down in the garden makes a dandy toad house, and the toads will reward you by eating their share of bugs. Courtesy Gardeners Supply Co.

mealybugs, whitefly, spider mites, earwigs, plant bugs, pear psyllids, tent caterpillars, and some other insects. Its very low toxicity makes it a good choice for enclosed greenhouses. Safer is also developing organic herbicide and fungicide products.

Diatomaceous Earth

This is a relative newcomer that is sometimes called Kieselguhr or Tripoli. It is a powder, safe for people to handle, that is made up of the ground fossilized remains of a form of

The botanical insecticide pyrethrum is derived from the pyrethrum chrysanthemum (*Chrysanthemum cinerariifolium*).

bage worm, asparagus beetle, webworm, and many more.

Be sure to purchase the correct type of diatomaceous earth (commonly sold under the trade name Permaguard); the kind of diatomaceous earth used in swimming pools is useless for pest control because it lacks sharp edges.

Bt and Milky Spore Disease

These are a form of germ warfare on pests. *Bacillus thuringiensis* (Bt) has been one of my favorites for years, since it attacks only insects in their larval stage but does so very effectively. In the lawn this means webworms, armyworms, and some cutworms. Bt will also kill tent caterpillars and the gypsy moth in its larval stage. In the garden, it kills tomato hornworms and cabbage worms. It is often sold under the trade name Dipel.

Milky spore disease, or *Bacillus popilliae*, attacks the grubs of Japanese, May, and June beetles. It is sold under the trade name Doom, among others. Once it has been sprayed on, an application should last several years. It does not harm earthworms.

Organic Pesticides

Rotenone, pyrethrum, sabadilla, and ryania are all extracts of plants. **Rotenone** is from the roots of derris and cubé. It is sometimes found in pet stores, since it is used to control pet parasites. It is a stomach and contact poison that kills beetles, aphids, loopers, thrips, and other bugs, but it also kills bees and is toxic to fish.

Pyrethrum comes from the seeds of the pyrethrum chrysanthemum (*Chrysanthemum cinerariifolium*), and is used to knock down and

sea algae called *diatoms*. To bugs, these sharp silicon particles are like crawling across razor blades, puncturing their shells and causing death by dehydration. It does not harm earthworms, although soft-bodied pests, including slugs, are vulnerable. It can be used on vegetables up to the day of harvest. When mixed with pyrethrins, which knock down flying insects, it controls aphids, leafhoppers, whitefly, Colorado potato beetle, cabbage looper, cab-

stun flying insects. Rotenone and pyrethrum are often found mixed with each other and with other compounds like diatomaceous earth and insecticidal soap.

Sabadilla has been in use for hundreds of years. It comes from a tropical lily and is used for its alkaloids, which attack the nervous system of adult bugs and cause paralysis and death. It is a fairly broad-spectrum pesticide and can be used on vegetables. For the lawn, it will kill chinch bugs, aphids, grasshoppers, and other adult insects, but it also kills bees.

Ryania is extracted from the powdered roots of a South American shrub. It may be hard to find. It is used against leaf-chewing insects, the corn borer, and on apple trees against the codling moth.

The advantage of the organics is the fact that they break down quickly and do not leave harmful residues. To avoid killing bees, apply them after sundown, when the bees have returned to their hives. Follow instructions when using these pesticides; they may be organic, but they are also very potent. They may kill beneficial insects like ladybugs and lacewings.

Parasitic Nematodes

Nematodes are microscopic, eel-like worms that live in the soil. They may be the most abundant form of life on earth. Parasitic nematodes kill grubs. They are sold in a gel form and sprayed on.

CHAPTER 12

GROUND COVERS
AND ORNAMENTAL GRASSES

ONE OF THE MOST interesting areas on my property is a steep hillside that, in season, is a beautiful glade covered with the orange blossoms of daylilies. Out of season it is a thick but still attractive mat of foliage that holds the bank in place. It is a wild area and is never fertilized.

The little turnaround circle in my driveway sports a thick, healthy bed of petunias every year. I planted the petunias several years ago. Every fall they go to seed and come back every spring with little or no maintenance. These plants that reseed themselves are what I call "volunteers." They show up whether you want them to or not. One of the oddball, but very useful ground covers, is the herb dill weed. Once heavily seeded in an area, it reseeds itself year after year. Grown in the right spot, it is both visually interesting and a source of either fresh dill leaves or dill heads for pickling. It might not be great in the front yard, but it could be perfect out behind the garage.

These are good examples of three reasons

for using ground covers: they provide interesting variety in a landscape; they often thrive in problem areas; and they may be maintenance-free. My guess is that nature created my lily bank, probably beginning when a farmer cleaned some daylilies out of another area and dumped them over the bank.

In fact, in many areas wildflowers are nature's ground cover: the daylily, the black-eyed Susan, the California poppy, the bluet of the East, the vetches, violets, and the beautiful bunchberry of the northern woods, to name just a few. I have transplanted wild ferns to provide an interesting ground cover on the cool and shady north sides of buildings. Wild mint will thrive and take over in damp areas. Wild thyme will flourish in poor, played-out soil, and smells good when you run a mower through it from time to time.

Too much shade is another reason for choosing a ground cover over grass. Many grasses are shade-tolerant, but if you can't get one to grow, you can always use a ground cover.

Ground covers are often used on problem areas where grass is difficult or impossible to grow, or where a colorful, low-maintenance planting is desired. This crown vetch cascades over a sloping lawn under a utility pole.

I use ground covers in shady areas under evergreens and shrubs where grass won't survive, and in ledgy, rocky, or terraced spots where it is impossible to mow.

You might choose a ground cover simply to provide a mass of color or texture in contrast to the lawn. Sometimes ground covers form a border between the lawn and taller shrubs that border a property. Some, like hosta, can be used in beds to outline sidewalks or walkways. Ground covers of native plants can also be the answer in areas where drought conditions make a lawn difficult to maintain. Plants like sedum thrive in poor soil, tolerate heat, resist drought, and will grow in every climate zone in the United States.

I plant ground covers in the spring here in the North, but in warmer climates they can be planted at any time as long as they are kept well watered. In warm climates, I would prefer to plant in the fall to take advantage of moderate weather and winter rains.

Choosing Ground Covers

Ground covers come back year after year, so it pays to make sure that you're getting one that is well suited to the location. Many have attractive blossoms, and they come in all shapes, sizes, and foliage colors. Here is a guide to some of the more common ones, and a few that I like because they are uncommon. Since they sometimes can be more reliable than common names, botanical names are given here for times when you're ordering plants from a catalog or nursery.

Ajuga, Carpet Bugleweed

(*Ajuga reptans*). Ajuga grows fast and likes the shady areas where grass is hard to grow. The foliage is about four inches high and different varieties have different-colored foliage, although all produce a blue flower late in the spring. Some foliage is purple to bronze, while others are burgundy, white, and cream. It is also used for borders and rock gardens. Plants are set about a foot apart.

Bird's-Foot Trefoil

(*Lotus corniculatus*). See Crown Vetch.

Bishop's Weed, Snow-on-the-Mountain

(*Aegopodium podagraria*). This is a very useful ground cover here in the North because it is very hardy and will grow in both partial sun and shade. It is often used as a foundation planting in shady areas. Foliage is green, with creamy white edges. It grows to about 10 inches and spreads rapidly. It sends up a white flower stalk in early summer. Plants set 15 inches apart will fill in quickly.

White Clover

(*Trifolium repens*). This is the clover that produces a small, white blossom. When heavily seeded, it makes a very attractive and hardy ground cover that will smother anything else that tries to get established. It reseeds itself every year.

Crown Vetch

(*Coronilla varia*). Along with bird's-foot trefoil (*Lotus corniculatus*), crown vetch is an excellent choice for erosion control on steep banks. In fact, the two are sometimes sold together as an erosion-control mix. The trick is to hold them in place until they get established; so if you have a real problem area, try annual ryegrass seed in combination with crown vetch and/or trefoil. Crown vetch grows in a dense, two- to three-foot-high mass that has pink flowers in the summer. It is grown from seed or from crowns, which are set 18 inches to two feet apart, for about 25 to 100 square feet. Bird's-foot trefoil grows to about 15 inches, has yellow flowers, and will tolerate heavy, wet soils. It, too, is grown from crowns and seeds. Both can be grown in all but the hottest parts of the United States.

Dichondra

(*Dichondra micrantha*). This is a favorite southern ground cover that does well where temperatures don't drop below 25°F (4°C). It forms a thick, green carpet of rounded, slightly heart-shaped leaves that can be mowed to about one and one-half inches. It does not need a lot of mowing. It is not good for traveled areas. While attractive, it unfortunately can provide a cozy home for snails, slugs, cutworms, and flea beetles. If weeds get started in dichondra, they can be hard to get out, which is why it is often kept mowed short.

Ferns

There are many varieties of ferns. I have used them as foundation plantings in shady, moist areas where everything else fails. They have a wild sort of jungle appeal that works well in naturalized areas. They like a lot of humus in the soil. Here in Vermont, fiddlehead ferns are harvested and cooked like vegetables early in spring, when the emerging shoot is still curled up and looks like the head of a fiddle.

Hosta, Funkia

(*Hosta* spp.). For some reason I remember hosta as the plant that bordered the sidewalk to a local church when I was a boy. Hosta grows from a clump and sends up a stalk of bell-shaped flowers that range in color from purple to white, depending upon the variety. They are often used in borders, edgings, and around the base of trees. Partial shade is best. The largest varieties, like blue giant, can get up to two feet tall. There are several varieties with very different leaf colorings, ranging from pale green with ivory to deep blue-green. They should be planted from two to two-and-a-half feet apart. They are very hardy.

Lily-of-the-Valley

(*Convallaria majalis*). I suspect nearly every old home has a patch of lily-of-the-valley somewhere around its foundation. Fond of shade, its dark green, upright leaves grow to about eight inches and conceal a stalk of small, white, sweet-smelling flowers shaped like bells. It likes well-drained soil. It spreads fast and grows in almost all climate zones.

Golden Moneywort, Creeping Charlie

(*Lysimachia nummularia*). Penny-shaped leaves form along trailing vines, which produce a yellow flower in summer. They plants are vigorous and good for holding banks. The trailing foliage will cascade over walls when planted along terraces. Also used in hanging baskets and window boxes, this plant prefers sun or partial shade.

Ground covers offer home landscapers a symphony of shapes, sizes, and colors from which to choose. This swath of eastern ground cover plants includes, in the background, left to right, clintonia, wild ginger, and bunchberry. In the foreground are wintergreen and partridgeberry.

Pachysandra, Spurge

(*Pachysandra terminalis*). I recommend growing pachysandra under pine trees because it likes both shade and acid soil. It might yellow in the sun. It forms dense mats of shiny green foliage about six to eight inches high. Good uses are for bare spots along evergreen hedges, terraces, and steep banks, and for edging shrub and flower borders. Start plants 12 to 15 inches apart.

Periwinkle, Myrtle

(*Vinca minor*). Forms a solid mat of evergreen foliage about eight inches tall, and produces a bright blue flower late in spring. This popular ground cover will grow in semi-shade and shaded areas, and can be used under trees and shrubs where grass won't grow. Good in most climate zones except along the Gulf Coast.

Plumbago, Leadwort

(*Plumbago auriculata*). This is a very adaptable ground cover that grows in sun or shade, to about 10 inches, and produces blue flowers from midsummer until frost. Planted 12 to 15 inches apart, it fills in fast with dark green foliage on wiry stems. It should be cut back for winter.

Sedum, Stonecrop

(*Sedum* spp.). There are so many sizes and colors of sedum it is hard to believe they are all part of the same genus. They can range from gold to bright red, and grow from four or five to as much as 18 to 24 inches tall. They are creepers that fill in rapidly and like hot, dry weather. That's when they bloom. Sedum might grow where grass won't. Plant from 12 to 24 inches apart, depending upon the variety. It prefers sun or light shade.

Winter Creeper

(*Euonymus radicans*). This plant grows along the ground, as its name suggests, but it can also be trained up as a vine to about 30 feet. It will stand full sun or shade, and is very hardy and dense. Green foliage turns purplish as fall sets in. Plant 18 to 24 inches apart. As a ground cover, it is 12 to 18 inches high. It can also be grown on walls and fences.

Oddballs, Wild Things, and Ornamental Grasses

Wild Thyme

(*Thymus serpyllum*). For folks with worn-out soil who pretty much plan to avoid lawn maintenance, as in the case of country summer places, wild thyme can be seeded over bald areas or transplanted as clumps. It might not take hold in damp or shady spots, but where it does take hold it is tough and doesn't need to be mowed. If you do mow it, though, it will produce tiny flowers and smell good, assuming you like the smell of thyme. It even gives off its fragrance when you walk on it.

Sweet Woodruff

(*Galium odoratum*). This is another ground cover that smells good, but this one grows in partially shaded, moist areas. It produces white flowers in the spring, which are traditionally used to make May wine. Set plants about a foot apart, or a little less.

Wildflowers

Wildflower seed mixes for a variety of conditions are available from mail-order catalogs and garden centers. In the country, a wildflower meadow will make city dwellers sell their condos. Here's one idea — seed with wildflowers after a construction project to cover the bare earth. One of the best wildflower meadows I have seen was created around a new pond, instead of reseeding with grass.

Transplanting wildflowers should be done only after checking with state officials to find out which species, if any, are protected in your area. There are a couple of secrets to success in transplanting wildflowers. First, I always try to match conditions for the transplants. If you have growing and soil conditions at home that match the ones in which the wildflower is found, it is worth a try to transplant. I transplant into plastic bags, taking enough of the surrounding soil to make a small bed. Don't let the roots dry out. Start with small areas. Don't be afraid to mix the plants up, if that's the way you observed them growing in the wild. Some possibilities for wildflower ground covers include:

Bluets

(*Hedyotis caerulea*). Also called Quaker ladies and innocence. They grow in low mats in a variety of conditions. You can always spot them because of their small, four-petaled flowers, which

The effective use of native wildflowers and ornamental grasses can create a beautiful, low-maintenance landscape — whether in a dry meadow or around the fringes of a pond.

range in color from white to light blue and have a yellow eye. Divide plants to bring some home. They will spread slowly into large beds.

Bunchberry

(*Cornus canadensis*). In the fall, the bright red bunches of berries and dark green foliage will remind you of holly. In the summer, a white flower forms in the center of a cluster of six leaves. Bunchberry likes cool, moist, shady spots and very acid soil that is rich in humus. Unless you can duplicate its growing conditions, you won't have much luck. But if you can, divide plants to propagate them.

Wild Ginger

(*Asarum canadense*). You may find these plants around very old cellar holes, because their roots were once used by our forebears as a ginger substitute. The leaves are heart-shaped and the stalks are fuzzy, with a brown flower near the ground. They grow to about eight inches. If you're not sure you've found the right plant, crush a piece of root and smell it. It grows very densely in full shade.

Wild Lily-of-the-Valley

(*Maianthemum canadense*). These are like the domestic variety (*Convallaria majalis*), except that the flowers look more like white tufts than a stalk of white bells.

Most of the wild ground covers I have mentioned are familiar here in the Northeast. A book of wildflowers that covers species native to your region of the country is a good starting point for your own investigations.

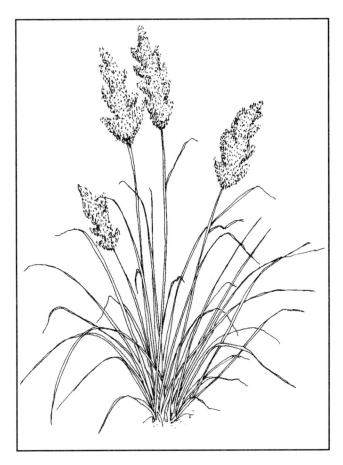

Pampas grass *(Cortaderia selloana)*

Ornamental Grasses

I think the first time I realized that a trimmed lawn or a hayfield was not just grass was when I noticed big, round clumps of grass growing on an island in a stream near home. Growing there in its wild state, I recognized that grass could be interesting for its own sake, just because of the way it grew and was shaped.

Grasses, which in warmer climates can include the bamboos, have a huge range of shapes and colors. Some produce plumes that look

Fountain grass *(Pennesetum selaceum)*

like silver horsetails or cotton candy. Others have leaves that are bright yellow or blood red. Some grow in mounds, while others grow taller than a basketball player and can be used as a privacy screen. Some are annuals (grow for only one season, then die), some are perennials (come back year after year), and some grow as perennials in the South and as annuals in the North.

If you can't find information or a selection at your local garden center, many of the mail-order seed catalogs carry a variety of ornamen-tal grasses. Among them are Park Seed, Miller Nurseries, Thompson & Morgan, and Jung Seeds.

Here is a sample of what you can expect to find:

Blue Fescue

(Festuca ovina ranan glauca). Grows in 10-inch blue clumps that look like a hedgehog, or something out of a science fiction story. Full sun, dry soil, and good drainage are required. Blue fescue is a new introduction and can be used as either a border or a ground cover.

Fountain Grass

(Pennisetum setaceum). Rich green foliage two feet high is topped in late summer with plumes that range from white to purple to copper. Also available in a shorter dwarf variety, an annual.

Morning Light

(Miscanthus cultivars). First cultivated in Japan, landscape architects use this grass in their designs because its white-bordered leaves catch the light and give it a kind of glow. It grows in clumps four to five feet high. It flowers in late summer and is hardy.

Pampas Grass

(Cortaderia selloana). Tall clumps grows stems that may reach 10 feet in height, and are topped with an ivory plume. These can be dried as an indoor decoration. There is also a pink variety. It grows as an annual in the North.

Ribbon Grass

(Phalaris arundinacea var. *picta)*. This old-fash-ioned ornamental spreads rapidly and produces

18- to 30-inch-tall, green-and-white-striped leaves. Easy to grow, even in poor soil, it enjoys full sun.

Zebra Grass

(*Miscanthus sinensis* 'Zebrinus'). Zebra grass grows up to eight feet tall, producing leaves with gold and green stripes running across the leaf. It also produces pink or beige plumes, and prefers full sun.

You can tell from some of the common names given to varieties of ornamental grasses (animated oats, quaking grass, squirrel-tail grass, foxtail) that they are often grown for the beauty of their plumes and how they play in the wind. If you really develop a passion for ornamental grasses, the best selections I have seen come from Monrovia Nursery in California (call, toll-free, 1-800-999-9321 for information). Monrovia is a wholesale nursery only.

APPENDIX

SOURCE LIST

Biological Gardening Material Suppliers

The following suppliers produce and/or distribute beneficial insects, tools, or other material for biological pest control, composting, and soil enhancement. Also consult extension services for recommendations and local suppliers.

Association of Applied Insect
    Ecologists
100 North Winchester Boulevard
Suite 260
Santa Cruz, CA 95050
    Beneficial insects

Bio-Control Co.
P.O. Box 337
57A Zink Road
Berry Creek, CA 95916
    Beneficial insects

Bio-Resources
P.O. Box 902
1210 Birch Street
Santa Paula, CA 93060
    Beneficial insects

Dyna-Prep, Inc.
2215 Broadway
Yankton, SD 57078
    Diatomaceous earth

Fairfax Biological Lab, Inc.
Clinton Corners, NY 12514
    Milky spore powder

The Fertrell Co.
P.O. Box 265
Bainbridge, PA 17502
    Fertilizers and soil amendments

Francis Laboratories
1551 East Lafayette
Detroit, MI 48207
    Natural fertilizers

Green Earth Organics
9422 144th Street East
Puyallup, WA 98373-6686
    Natural lawn care products

Green Pro Services
380 South Franklin Street
Hempstead, NY 11550
    Natural gardening products

Growing Naturally
P.O. Box 54
149 Pine Lane
Pineville, PA 18946
    Natural gardening products

Mellinger's
2310 West South Range Road
Lima, OH 44452-9731
    Fertilizers, soil conditioners, and soil amendments

Natural Gardening Research Center
Highway 48
P.O. Box 149
Sunman, IN 47041
    Beneficial insects and supplies for organic gardening

Natural Gardening Research Center
Highway 48
P.O. Box 149
Sunman, IN 47041
    Natural gardening products

Nitron Industries
4605 Johnson Road
P.O. Box 1447
Fayetteville, AR 72702
    Organic gardening supplies, including natural fertilizers and soil enhancers

Ohio Earth Food, Inc.
13737 Duquette Avenue, Northeast
Hartville, OH 44632
    Natural gardening materials, specializing in sea products

Perma-Guard
1701 East Elwood Street
Phoenix, AZ 85040
    Diatomaceous earth

Reuter Labs, Inc.
8540 Natural Way
Manassas Park, VA 22111
    Natural pest controls

Rincon-Vitove Insectaries
P.O. Box 475
Rialto, CA 92376
    Beneficial insects

Ringer Corporation
9959 Valley View Road
Eden Prairie, MN 55344
    Organic soil amendments, beneficial insects, garden tools, and irrigation equipment

Safer, Inc.
60 William Street
Wellesley, MA 02181
Pest controls, natural soaps, and natural herbicides

Super Natural American
Distributing Company
13906 Ventura Boulevard
Sherman Oaks, CA 91423
Natural fertilizers

Unique Insect Control
5504 Sperry Drive
Citrus Heights, CA 95621
Beneficial insects

Zook & Ranck, Inc.
RD 2, Box 243
Gap, PA 17527
Fertilizer and soil amendments

Cooperative Extension Services

United States

Alabama

Alabama A & M University
Normal, AL 35762

Auburn University
Auburn, AL 36849

Tuskegee Institute
Tuskegee, AL 36088

Alaska

University of Alaska
Fairbanks, AK 99775

Arizona

University of Arizona
Tucson, AZ 85721

Arkansas

Extension Administration
P.O. Box 391
Little Rock, AR 72203

University of Arkansas
Fayetteville, AR 72701

California

Kearney Agricultural Center
Parlier, CA 93648

University of California
College of Natural Resources
Berkeley, CA 94720

University of California
College of Agriculture and
Environmental Sciences
Davis, CA 95616

University of California
College of Natural and
Agricultural Sciences
Riverside, CA 92502

Colorado

Colorado State University
College of Agricultural Sciences
Fort Collins, CO 80523

Fruita Research Center
Box 786
Grand Junction, CO 81502

Connecticut

Connecticut Agricultural
Experiment Station
P.O. Box 1106
New Haven, CT 06504

University of Connecticut
Storrs, CT 06268

Delaware

Delaware State College
Dover, DE 19901

University of Delaware
College of Agricultural Sciences
Newark, DE 19711

District of Columbia

University of the District
of Columbia
Washington, DC 20005

Florida

Florida A & M University
Tallahassee, FL 32307

University of Florida
College of Agriculture
Gainesville, FL 32611

Georgia

Fort Valley State College
School of Agriculture
Fort Valley, GA 31030

University of Georgia
College of Agriculture
Athens, GA 30602

Hawaii

University of Hawaii
Honolulu, HI 96822

Idaho

University of Idaho
College of Agriculture
Moscow, ID 83843

Illinois

University of Illinois
College of Agriculture
Urbana, IL 61801

Indiana

Purdue University
School of Agriculture
West Lafayette, IN 47907

Iowa

Iowa State University
College of Agriculture
Ames, IA 50011

Kansas

Kansas State University
College of Agriculture
Manhattan, KS 66506

Kentucky

Kentucky State University
Frankfort, KY 40601

University of Kentucky
College of Agriculture
Lexington, KY 40506

Louisiana

Louisiana State University
Baton Rouge, LA 70893

Southern University and
A & M College
Baton Rouge, LA 70813

Maine

University of Maine
College of Agriculture
Orono, ME 04469

Maryland

University of Maryland
College of Agriculture
College Park, MD 20742

University of Maryland
Eastern Shore
Department of Agriculture
Princess Anne, MD 21853

Massachusetts

University of Massachusetts
College of Agriculture
Amherst, MA 01003

Michigan

Michigan State University
College of Agriculture and
Natural Resources
East Lansing, MI 48824

Minnesota

University of Minnesota
College of Agriculture and
Natural Resources
St. Paul, MN 55108

Mississippi

Alcorn State College
Lorman, MS 39096

Mississippi State University
College of Agriculture
Mississippi State, MS 39762

Missouri

Lincoln University
Jefferson City, MS 65101

University of Missouri
College of Agriculture
Columbia, MO 65211

Montana

Montana State University
College of Agriculture
Bozeman, MT 59717

Nebraska

University of Nebraska
Institute of Agriculture and
Natural Resources
Lincoln, NE 68583

Nevada

University of Nevada
College of Agriculture
Reno, NV 89557

New Hampshire

University of New Hampshire
College of Agriculture
Durham, NH 03824

New Jersey

Rutgers State University
College of Agriculture
New Brunswick, NJ 08903

New Mexico

New Mexico State University
College of Agriculture
Las Cruces, NM 88003

New York

Cornell University
College of Agriculture
Ithaca, NY 14853

New York State Agricultural
Experiment Station
Geneva, NY 14456

North Carolina

North Carolina A & T
State University
School of Agriculture
Greensboro, NC 27411

North Carolina State University
College of Agriculture
Raleigh, NC 27695

North Dakota

North Dakota State University
of Agriculture and Applied Science
State University Station
Fargo, ND 58105

Ohio

Ohio State University
College of Agriculture
Columbus, OH 43210

Oklahoma

Langston University
Agricultural Research and Extension
P.O. Box 730
Langston, OK 73050

Oklahoma State University
College of Agriculture
Stillwater, OK 74078

Oregon

Oregon State University
College of Agriculture
Corvallis, OR 97331

Pennsylvania

Pennsylvania State University
College of Agriculture
University Park, PA 16802

Rhode Island

University of Rhode Island
Kingston, RI 02881

South Carolina

Clemson University
College of Agricultural Sciences
Clemson, SC 29631

South Carolina State College
Orangeburg, SC 29115

South Dakota

South Dakota State University
College of Agriculture
Brookings, SD 57007

Tennessee

Tennessee State University
School of Agriculture
Nashville, TN 37203

University of Tennessee
Institute of Agriculture
Knoxville, TN 37901

Texas

Texas A & M University
College of Agriculture
College Station, TX 77843

Utah

Utah State University
College of Agriculture
Logan, UT 84322

Vermont

University of Vermont
College of Agriculture
Burlington, VT 05405

Virginia

Virginia Polytechnic Institute
and State University
College of Agriculture
Blacksburg, VA 24061

Washington

Washington State University
College of Agriculture
Pullman, WA 99164

West Virginia

West Virginia University
College of Agriculture
Morgantown, WV 26506

Wisconsin

University of Wisconsin
College of Agriculture
Madison, WI 53706

Wyoming

University of Wyoming
College of Agriculture
Laramie, WY 82071

United States Territories

Guam

University of Guam
College of Agriculture
Mangilao UOG Station, Guam 96923

Puerto Rico

University of Puerto Rico
College of Agricultural Sciences
Mayaguez, PR 00708

Virgin Islands

College of the Virgin Islands
Agricultural Experiment Station
RR 2, Box 10,000
St. Croix, VI 00850

Canada

Alberta

Alberta Tree Nursery and
Horticultural Center
RR #6, 17507 Fort Road
Edmonton, AB T5B 4K3

British Columbia

Hort-line
University of British Columbia
Botanical Gardens
6804 Southwest Marine Drive
Vancouver, BC V6T 1W5

Manitoba

Horticulture Section
Soils and Crops Branch
Manitoba Horticulture
908-401 York Avenue
Winnipeg, MB R3C 0P8

New Brunswick

New Brunswick Department
of Agriculture
Information Section
Research Station
P.O. Box 6000
Fredericton, NB E3B 5H1

Newfoundland

Department of Forestry and
Agriculture
Provincial Agriculture Building
Brookfield Road
P.O. Box 8700
St. John's, NF A1B 4J6

Nova Scotia

Nova Scotia Agricultural College
P.O. Box 550
Truro, NS B2N 5E3

Kentville Agricultural Center
Kentville, NS B4N 1J5

Ontario

Master Gardener's Program
(over 20 offices, for the nearest
location, consult the Ontario
Ministry of Agriculture
and Food listed in your
telephone directory)

Prince Edward Island

Prince Edward Island
Department of Agriculture
Research Station
P.O. Box 1600
Charlottetown, PE C1A 7N3

Quebec

Ministere de l'Agriculture,
des Pecheries et de l'Alimentation
(Agriculture, Fisheries and Food)
Direction des Communications
200-A Chemin Ste-Foy
Quebec, QC G1R 4X6

Saskatchewan

University of Saskatchewan
Extension and Community Relations
Saskatoon, SK S7N 0W0

Landscaping Institutes

California State Polytechnic
University
Institute for Environmental Design
3801 West Temple Avenue
Pomona, CA 91768

Iowa State University
Design Research Institute
134 College of Design
Ames, IA 50011

Landscape Architecture Foundation
1733 Connecticut Avenue NW
Washington, DC 20009

The Lawn Institute
County Line Road
P.O. Box 108
Pleasant Hill, TN 38578-0108

Louisiana State University
Computer Aided Design
& Geographic Information
Systems Laboratory
Room 216, College of Design
Baton Rouge, LA 70803

University of Arizona
Arizona Agricultural Experiment
Station
Tucson, AZ 85721

University of Guelph Arboretum
Guelph, ON N1G 2W1
Canada

University of Kentucky
Kentucky Agricultural Experiment
Station
Agricultural Sciences Building North
Lexington, KY 40546

University of Michigan
Nichols Arboretum
Ann Arbor, MI 48109-1115

University of Pennsylvania
Morris Arboretum
9414 Meadowbrook Avenue
Philadelphia, PA 19118

University of Wisconsin
Wisconsin Agricultural Experiment
Station
140 Agricultural Hall
Madison, WI 53706

Washington State University
College of Agriculture and
Home Economics Research Center
Pullman, WA 99164

Tool and Equipment Suppliers

The following companies manufacture
and distribute gardening equipment.
Write for catalogs and information re-
garding local dealers.

Amerind MacKissic, Inc.
P.O. Box 111
Parker Ford, PA 19457
Large power garden tools

Country Home Products
Ferry Road
P.O. Box 89
Charlotte, VT 05445
*Mowers, trimmers, clippers, and
various garden tools*

Garden Way, Inc.
102nd Street & 9th Avenue
Troy, NY 12179-0009
*Mowers, rotary tillers, and various
garden tools*

Gardener's Supply Co.
128 Intervale Road
Burlington, VT 05401
Greenhouse kits and garden tools

Kemp Company
160 Koser Road
Lititz, PA 17543
Shredders, chippers, compost-tumblers, and other garden supplies

Kinco Manufacturing
Dept. 7702
170 N. Pascal
St. Paul, MN 55104
Heavy power mowers

Mainline
P.O. Box 526, Dept. GM190
London, OH 43140
Rotary tillers, mowers, and other power tools

Mantis Manufacturing Co.
1458 County Line Road
Huntingdon Valley, PA 19006
Lawn and garden equipment including tillers, chippers, and mowers

The Plow & Hearth
301 Madison Road
P.O. Box 830
Orange, VA 22960

Smith & Hawken
25 Corte Madera
Mill Valley, CA 94941
Tools, ornaments, and planting stock

INDEX

Page references in *italics* indicate illustrations. **Boldface** references indicate charts.